Spirit of the Orchestra

Helen Wallace

Sponsored by

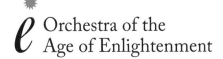
Orchestra of the
Age of Enlightenment

ISBN 0-9554024-0-9
ISBN 978-0-9554024-0-1

Published by The Orchestra of the Age of Enlightenment 2006
© The Orchestra of the Age of Enlightenment 2006

Orchestra of the Age of Enlightenment
4th Floor, 9 Irving Street, London, WC2H 7AH
Telephone. 020 7321 6330 Facsimile. 020 7930 8686
Email. info@oae.co.uk
Website. www.oae.co.uk

Contents

This book is dedicated to the memory of Tim Mason,
and to every musician who has performed with the
Orchestra of the Age of Enlightenment.

'We shall never become musicians unless we understand the
ideals of temperance, fortitude, liberality and magnificence.'

Plato

Preface

Nicholas Kenyon

The founding of the Orchestra of the Age of Enlightenment in 1986 was one of the absolutely decisive moments in British musical life. It may turn out to be comparable in its significance to the formation of the London Symphony Orchestra back in 1904, for the parallels are quite close: in both cases orchestral players were seizing back command of their own destiny, saying that they were the best people to organise their own lives, both managerially and artistically.

The growing public enthusiasm for period-instrument orchestral performance was little more than a decade old in 1986, and it had taken off with astonishing speed, thanks to the pioneers to whom the early music movement owes so much. The success coincided with a thirst, especially in the record companies, for bold new interpretations of Baroque and Classical music, and it grew with the arrival and development of the CD, for which everything had to be re-recorded. Early music was in luck, and soon it was up there in the charts with Pavarotti, players were busy and the movement was thriving.

But although the fame of the first director-led groups helped create public taste, there was perhaps an under-acknowledgement at the time that it was the players who had taken the risks. They had spent long hours mastering new-old techniques and new-old instruments, often to the amused contempt of colleagues. Yes, it had brought rewards, but by the mid-1980s the time was ripe for a new development, and it seems in retrospect clear that, especially in London, the home of player-led orchestras, this could take the form of a self-governing orchestra in which the musicians themselves made the decisions.

This offered the chance for the new orchestra to expand the range of its artistic relationships, and this was critical in ensuring the early triumphs of the OAE. Conductors who had not previously worked with period instruments were attracted in, and the period-instrument repertory expanded by leaps and bounds. The epoch-making Mozart *Idomeneo* of 1987 with Simon Rattle, so nearly cancelled for lack of money, turned out to be the way into Glyndebourne and Mozart, and thence to the currently dazzling Handel operas there: a central relationship. The wonderful Verdi operas and then the Requiem with Mark Elder, romantic repertory brought blazingly to life by Charles Mackerras, Haydn with Sigiswald Kuijken, the smaller player-led ventures, the Beethoven symphony cycle: all helped the Orchestra to develop and nurture a wide range of flexible performing styles for different repertory.

All I can say is that from a listener's perspective the OAE has provided some of my most stimulating musical experiences of the last 21 years and more recently at the BBC Proms: the experience of Bach's B minor Mass in 2000, Beethoven's *Fidelio*, the huge risky adventure of Wagner's *Das Rheingold*, and the new Robert Levin completion of the Mozart C minor Mass have all been outstanding highlights.

The OAE needs to go on being revolutionary, to go on challenging our perceptions and our expectations. It won't be easy in a musical world which is changing rapidly and the old certainties no longer apply, but the players of the OAE have the commitment, the flexibility and the imagination to adapt and develop. It's been great so far: Happy birthday!

Nicholas Kenyon

Beginnings: 1986-1987

In these two short years a new period instrument orchestra was formed with a radical open-door policy: open to more than a hundred instrumental players who could choose to become members, and open to conductors both from the modern symphony orchestral world and period specialists from the Continent. Between 1986 and 1987 the Age of Enlightenment, as it was initially called, worked with Sigiswald Kuijken, Gustav Leonhardt, Charles Mackerras, Roger Norrington and Simon Rattle. By the summer of 1987, there was a broadcast agreement with the BBC, a contract with Virgin Classics, plans for a major season at the South Bank Centre and Glyndebourne had invited the Orchestra to perform the next cycle of Da Ponte operas.

1985 Judith Hendershott takes up the challenge of creating a new orchestra.

1985 Catherine Mackintosh, then leader of the Academy of Ancient Music, makes contact with Bankers Trust.

1986 Sigiswald Kuijken, the violinist director of the OAE's first concert.

1986 Roger Norrington conducts a Weber programme at the Queen Elizabeth Hall.

Photos: Annemie, Susan Benn, Hanya Chlala, Stuart Keegan

1987 Gustav Leonhardt directs a CPE Bach concert.

The first known picture of the OAE, published in 1987.

August 1987 'We have to do *Idomeneo*!'. Felix Warnock with Simon Rattle, whose performance was noted by Glyndebourne.

1987 Violinist Monica Huggett in the first OAE performances of the Brandenburg Concertos.

1987 Charles Mackerras conducts his first concert with the OAE.

Virgin Classics signed a deal in 1987. The first LP was Schubert's 9th Symphony with Charles Mackerras.

Concert posters from 1987.

Beginnings

CONCEPTION

It all began with a cancellation. Or, at least, a proposed cancellation. The Academy of Ancient Music (AAM) were due to perform a concert on 30 November 1985 at St. Margaret's, Westminster. The circumstances of the concert were somewhat unusual: for once Christopher Hogwood, founder and conductor of the AAM, was not directing. He had a date elsewhere and the Orchestra's manager, Judith Hendershott, in response to the players' enthusiasm, had booked Flemish Baroque violinist Sigiswald Kuijken instead. As the concert date approached it became clear it was going to incur a loss: the funding had fallen through. Catherine Mackintosh, leader of the Orchestra, did not want to lose the opportunity of performing with Kuijken and took matters into her own hands. She got in touch with a well-connected cousin of her husband's, Al Giloti, who worked at the American Bankers Trust Company, and asked to see the Head of Sponsorship. Enter Michael Rose, who offered a small amount of funding and lent his ear to some ideas Mackintosh and her colleagues had formulated about starting a new kind of orchestra. Judith Hendershott, who was by then already working out her notice with AAM, pushed forward with the concert, and suggested that Rose might like to meet some of the players afterwards…

One of the players who, by luck or design, found himself sitting next to Michael Rose at the post-concert dinner was bassoonist Felix Warnock. He takes up the story: 'We got talking – I had no idea who he was – but he seemed rather well-informed, and he started questioning me about how you got the right freelance players under the right roof. We got on to discussing problems, and I found myself articulating a vision for how a player-run orchestra could work.'

The problems he referred to derived from the structure of the Early Music scene at the time. A relatively small group of specialist freelance players was moving between several different ensembles, each the property of its founding director, Christopher Hogwood's Academy of Ancient Music, Trevor Pinnock's English Concert, John Eliot Gardiner's English Baroque Soloists and Roger Norrington's London Classical Players. 'We had arrived at a point in the mid-1980s,' recalls Warnock, 'when these founder-conductors were becoming rather famous. They were starting to get invitations to conduct abroad, and we felt the consequence would be a reduction in our work, despite the part we had played in putting them on the map in the first place.'

'We'd also become aware that there was a group of 'modern' conductors who wanted to have the experience of conducting period instruments but had no vehicle with which to work. A key member of that group was Simon Rattle, but there was also Charles Mackerras, who had done so much with Handel and Mozart already, and Mark Elder, who had been at Cambridge with another friend and colleague, the cellist Tim Mason. But, as none of the founding directors of the period bands wanted to let anyone else loose on their own ensembles, there was simply no orchestra in the world the modern lot could conduct.'

The third 'problem' was that there were some very eminent musicians on the Continent who had been doing pioneering work on performance style – including Gustav Leonhardt, Sigiswald Kuijken, Nikolaus Harnoncourt, Frans Brüggen and Ton Koopman – who rarely, if ever, came to

Michael Rose of Bankers Trust Company, who Catherine Mackintosh contacted in 1985. He funded the incorporation of the Orchestra, dreamed up a name and funded the first two concerts. His support was critical to the Orchestra's early success.

Top: the OAE rehearses in the Sheldonian in the early days
Below, from left: Founder members Tim Mason and Felix Warnock, who would become Chairman and Manager, discuss tactics with conductor Iván Fischer.

London and, if they did, it was with their own bands. Many of the British players had studied with these leading lights, and had even played in their orchestras, so were keen to invite them over to work on specific repertoire. But how could it be done within the existing structures?

'There was a flaw in the system,' remarks Warnock. 'Gradually it became clear that we had to do something, or nothing would change, the system had become arthritic and *we* needed to open it up, to enrich the musical life of London.' The small act of resistance to ensure the AAM concert got off the ground became the spur to further revolt.

A CHARMED LIFE

From the outside, London's Early Music scene could not have seemed less arthritic. Quite the opposite, it was a ferment of activity. Since the pioneering work of David Munrow from the late Sixties together with the founding of Trevor Pinnock's English Concert in 1972, there had been an explosion of performance of Baroque and early Classical repertoire on period instruments. No sooner was an ensemble created, than record labels fell over each other to initiate comprehensive recording projects: Decca's L'Oiseau-lyre backed Christopher Hogwood's AAM, Archiv took on John Eliot Gardiner's English Baroque Soloists and Pinnock's English Concert, and EMI Roger Norrington's London Classical Players, to name but four. The recording boom was to last until the early 1990s, and provided an important stream of work and income for the players. Says viola player Annette Isserlis, 'We led a charmed life. All the groups fitted their diaries around each other, so we got to do most of the recording sessions and concerts. It was a very rewarding time financially: a lot of us bought instruments on the money we made from recordings. I really feel for my students today, it is so much harder.'

Despite the level of activity, a staleness was setting in. Says violinist Marshall Marcus: 'As the 1980s progressed, the period instrument movement was becoming a victim of its own success – more quick recordings, more long haul tours, more success, less endeavour.' Players were beginning to feel part of a production line which affected their playing style, as Annette Isserlis describes: 'I felt we had got into in-grown habits, like leaving huge gaps before last notes, it was a mannerism that had grown out of groups directed from the harpsichord – there was that British thing of 'No, after you, no, after you.' Lead violinist Alison Bury also felt they needed to be shaken out of their ubiquitous, default 'Baroque' style of playing: 'There was an English way of playing that had become formulaic. It's hard to describe, but perhaps there was an over-familiarity setting in. Of course, we admired and respected the English directors enormously, nothing that came later could have been done without their drive and energy in the early 80s.'

The desire for change was also linked to the stage many had reached in their careers, as violinist Catherine Mackintosh explains: 'I was feeling it was time to develop musically. The idea of having different directors that we could choose depending on the repertoire was a great, liberating idea: it attracted the good players who wanted to carry on learning.' Interestingly, many of the players had just had children: it was a time of upheaval, a time for reassessing the nature and value of their performing lives.

These were the issues Felix Warnock discussed with Michael Rose, who took an unusually intense interest in the conversation. Still, it was a surprise when he rang Warnock the next morning to say that he been think-

Founder Member, viola player Annette Isserlis: 'We led a charmed life. All the groups fitted their diaries around each other, so we got to do most of the recording sessions and concerts. It was a very rewarding time financially.'

ing about the idea overnight and would like Felix to gather together a group of players to come and talk to some other people at Bankers Trust about the idea. Warnock rang around the players who had already been discussing the idea among themselves: he managed to reach leading clarinettist Antony Pay, Anthony Halstead, an expert exponent of natural horns, Marshall Marcus, who led the Orchestra of St. John's Smith Square, and had played in the BBC SO, the Orquesta Filarmonica de Caracas and the Endymion Ensemble among others, and Tim Mason, cellist of the London Fortepiano Trio, founder of the contemporary music group Capricorn, and principal cello of the English Baroque Soloists. As Warnock remarks, 'It was a miracle that we managed to assemble a group of very distinguished and very busy musicians. I think Michael Rose wanted to test the consensus, to see if I was just a lone crack-pot.' The other important individual to attend that first meeting was Judith Hendershott, who, newly released from her responsibilities with the AAM, was keen to drive forward this new idea. She would take it on seven days a week from that point onwards.

Marshall Marcus remembers it clearly, 'We had been talking about it for a while before this: I went along to the bank as one of the fascinated. Eventually, Tim, Felix and I became a bit of a gang of three. We were forever getting into corners to exchange ideas, to the point where, I suspect, it rather irritated others.'

The enthusiasm, expertise and entrepreneurial spirit of the musi-

The Orchestra in the early Nineties.

DEMOCRACY... OAE STYLE
BY MARSHALL MARCUS FOUNDER MEMBER

In the beginning was chaos... actually no, in the beginning with the OAE it was an age of reason. During the spring of 1986 a loose group of conspirators gathered together on the 12th floor of Bankers Trust in the City of London to debate how a new entity might be constructed ruled by equality and inclusiveness. Looking back now I see that most of us were still living in the 'Sixties' ('*stuck*' is, I believe, the favoured verb these days). We were probably about as naïve as you could be, yet the feeling of it was really rather wonderful and, unlike in most institutions, the residue of that wonder has actually never died but has in some respects strengthened as we have grown.

Chaos came later. Once the concerts began in earnest, the musical chairs also began. There was the prospect that this utopia might deliver not only great concerts but also some attractive career opportunties, and then the discussions on personnel began... and carried on. Many fractious orchestral meetings later something that we now choose to call a consensus arose, and we got back to the business of how to run an orchestra rather than trying to reinvent one every time we needed to discuss exchanging up bows for down bows.

The members still vote for those who might represent them on the various committees; players still 'jockey' for influence and the management still attempts to ensure that it protects the small distance required to manage. Meanwhile the elders and outside influences look on from a further, safer, distance. All familiar stuff. But there is still that bit of democracy in the beast, that curious English belligerent quality that helps us as an orchestra to retain the individuality and zest that makes our audience come back for more. Democracy... OAE style.

cians must have impressed Rose, who agreed to fund the start-up costs of a new orchestra and to pay for Hendershott to be its administrator. Over the course of the next eight months, several meetings were held on the 12th floor of Bankers Trust. The legal costs of incorporating the new ensemble as a charity were met and, crucially, money found for two initial concerts. Christopher Hogwood was not pleased. As far as he could see, a potentially important sponsor for the AAM had been hijacked by a breakaway group at a concert he had bankrolled. He later, famously, referred to the new orchestra as 'The Age of Embezzlement'. Warnock was mortified to discover the cause of Hogwood's antipathy, but quickly ascertained the accusation was hollow.

Jan Schlapp, Vice-Chairman of the OAE and principal viola player: 'To be honest, my first reaction was "Not *another* crazy idea." It was far too ambitious, far too difficult and it seemed unachievable, there was no money, nothing to sustain it.'

ANOTHER CRAZY IDEA

Viola player Jan Schlapp, wife of Tim Mason, remembers the day Tim came home from the first meeting. 'We had very little children at the time and I was knee-deep in nappies. Tim came in full of this idea to set up a new orchestra, "We're going to run it ourselves and we're not going to have a conductor.' The couple knew about setting up ensembles: Jan had been one of the founder members with John Lubbock of the Orchestra of St. John's Smith Square, while Tim had founded and was single-handedly running Capricorn. 'To be honest,' Jan remembers, 'My first reaction was "Oh my God! – not *another* crazy idea". It was far too ambitious, far too difficult – and it wasn't as if we had any spare time at all, and this would take more time, more effort. And it seemed unachievable, there was no money, nothing to sustain it.'

But Tim, it transpired, was to become perhaps the strongest driving force behind the enterprise and the Orchestra's first Chairman. Phones began to ring. 'Oh, there was definitely a sense of a rebellion,' remembers violinist Roy Mowatt, 'Marshall, Felix and Tim wanted to overthrow the rulers, the kings.' An invitation was sent out to players all over London and Hendershott began to ring round. Double Bass player Chi-chi Nwanoku remembers the call: 'Judy said "Would you like to be part of something where the players decide everything and we are not just under one person's thumb?". I signed up to it immediately. At the time the only other player-led chamber orchestra was the Chamber Orchestra of Europe.' Baroque flautist Lisa Beznosiuk and violinist Catherine Mackintosh also joined an early meeting to discuss how the Orchestra would be organised. One of the first tasks of the start-up group was to choose a name: 'A number of us had played with the Academy of St. Martin in the Fields, and the last thing we wanted was another unwieldy name!', recalls Warnock. Suggestions included Mr Handel's Orchestra, Children of Candide and the Amadeus Chamber Orchestra. Everyone voted and Michael Rose's idea came through: 'The Age of Enlightenment', at first without 'Orchestra' attached. Marshall Marcus has always thought of it in terms of Professor Roy Porter's concept of 'the long 18th Century. He looks at the key movements of the 18th Century as having begun in the late 17th Century and having moved right through into the 19th Century, which covers all our key repertoire periods.' Critics who were quick to point out that the band's repertoire had strayed out of bounds 'missed the whole point,' comments Michael Rose: 'the Age of Enlightenment was as much the late 1980s as it was the period of the core repertoire.' Looking back, it is the spirit of enquiry and empirical research embraced by Enlightenment ideals that has had a special reso-

Felix Warnock, bassoonist and founder member: 'Gradually it became clear that we had to do something or nothing would change. The system had become arthritic and we needed to open it up.'

nance for the founders of this project, and which has defined the character of the Orchestra.

ENLIGHTENMENT IDEALS

The original subscribers on the Orchestra's first Board in July 1986 included Marshall Marcus, Tony Halstead, John Hough, Lisa Beznosiuk, Tim Mason, Felix Warnock, Michael Rose and Mary (later Baroness) Warnock. They were later to be joined by David Frankel, a marketing guru from Coopers & Lybrand, and Christopher Lawrence, a keen amateur cellist who worked in the City and later ran the London Philharmonic Orchestra. He would go on to make a key introduction.

The original idea for the Age of Enlightenment embraced democratic ideals in their fullest sense. Anyone who wanted to could become a member of this new 'society', although they wouldn't necessarily be asked to play: 'It's so delightfully Enlightenment,' says Marcus now. 'You can just imagine a society like that being set up in the 18th Century. In fact it was the maddest form of orchestral membership you can imagine, and it took a lot of unpicking at a later date.'

Democracy was to inform the artistic direction of the Orchestra too: the Board devolved responsibility for concert planning to an Artistic Direction Committee (ADC) elected each year by the membership, a structure that has endured. One egalitarian ideal that survived in some form for many years was that everyone would be paid the same. Orchestras have sometimes been paired with the Catholic Church as being the most hierarchical institutions known to man. It wasn't long before the leaders were demanding more, and an exception was also made for trumpets. 'I don't think an orchestra, by its very nature', says one violinist, 'can be an egalitarian institution. There has to be mutual respect, yes, but not equality. The leader and the principals have to put in many more hours of preparation before even the first rehearsal.'

A mission statement written in the early days reveals many of the frustrations encountered by the musicians in their working lives at the time – all still current today: in order to attract the best period instrument players the Orchestra of the Age of Enlightenment was to:

'Avoid the dangers implicit in:
- playing as a matter of routine,
- pursuing exclusively commercial creative options,
- under-rehearsal,
- undue emphasis as imposed by a single music director,
- recording objectives being more important than creative objectives.'

This last one was significant: by the mid-1980s, the Early Music movement had in some respects become a creature of the recording industry. Because the recording projects aimed to cover the complete works of many composers, there was a drive not to repeat pieces. Says Warnock, 'It was absurd in terms of live performance, the idea that you could never go back on a piece of music was anti-musical. You need to build up and refine a repertoire and then come home to it.' There was also the small matter of a public being fed high quality, well-edited recordings in perfect acoustic settings, which bore little relation to their experience of the ensembles in the acoustically-compromised London halls. There they often encountered pinched sound, poor tuning and ensemble problems. Although the OAE would go on to make recordings, it was in the live and broadcast arena that it made its initial impact: in its first two years the BBC recorded every single concert, and has continued to have a strong relationship with the Orchestra.

THE INAUGURAL CONCERT

Judith Hendershott had set up an office in her flat in Blackheath and worked tirelessly to organise the Orchestra's future. 'It was daunting but exciting. I was doing the fixing, the press, marketing, programmes, everything. I was charged with commissioning the first logo which used an 18th Century typeface with a star shape: it may sound crazy, but in November 1985 Halley's Comet was passing over, and it seemed not only an auspicious sign but had a good Enlightenment connection.' The comet remains.

Oxford Town Hall, where the first OAE concert took place in June 1986.

The OAE's first concerts, in June 1986, were booked at Oxford's Town Hall and London's Queen Elizabeth Hall (QEH) as, somewhat incongruously, part of the Previn Music Festival. Michael Rose explains: 'Bankers Trust were already sponsoring the André Previn Festival, and I mentioned the formation of the Age of Enlightenment at one their planning meetings and the 'problem' of their first concert. John Bimson and Ian Maclay of the RPO looked at me askance. Sponsors were there to provide funding not to cast themselves in the role of artistic directors! However, once they had had an opportunity to see the A-list of players involved, they were enthusiastic and the date was generously given.'

Sigiswald Kuijken was to direct: 'That was no accident,' explains Marcus. 'It was his direction of the AAM concert in 1985 that had provided the impetus for the whole project. We realised then we could not leave it to the whim of a conductor whether or not we worked with talents like Sigiswald.' Flautist Lisa Beznosiuk remembers agonising over the programme: 'We were trying to make a statement: the programme was unusual and innovative, carefully thought-out to bridge the gap between the Baroque and Classical. There was a fantastic Telemann Overture Suite with two horns, Rameau's Suite from *Dardanus*, a symphony by Gossec and Haydn's Symphony 'La Poule'. Before the concert I was nervous in a new way: I think I cared almost too much about it.'

The care that had gone into the event did not go unnoticed: critics were unanimous in recognising something different and special about the Orchestra. Judith Hendershott and the Artistic Direction Committee had cleverly secured promises from many leading conductors by the time of this concert, which gave the launch an impressive fanfare: Simon Rattle, Charles Mackerras, Frans Brüggen, Gustav Leonhardt and Roger Norrington had already signed up. (They even rashly announced that Harnoncourt would work with them although in fact he never did.) The backing of Bankers Trust gave an added sheen to proceedings: it was quite some arrival. Robert Henderson in *The Daily Telegraph* noted the difference: 'the signs are that the performance of classical music on period instruments has finally come of age.' Hilary Finch of *The Times* hints at an impatience with the current debate over performing practice: 'Forty-five minutes and five acts worth of tingling music passed by in what seemed like quarter of an hour... could this at last be a group of musicians, neither specialists nor dilettante, unscathed by political wrangling and able to make an audience forget for a moment whether or not the flutes are made of wood, and whether the direction comes from baton or bow?' Nicholas Kenyon in the *Observer* was impressed but sounded a warning note: 'If the results continue to be as brilliantly virtuosic as in this... they will have little to fear from the competition. But such a self-governing orchestra will need large financial resources and a very strong artistic character, and neither of these grows on trees.'

SIR ROGER NORRINGTON'S FIRST CONCERT

After the success of the Kuijken programme, the members of the new ADC volunteered hours of their time to work with Judith Hendershott on plans for the next two or three years. Five months elapsed before the next concert, but it was yet again a musically significant event, this time a whole evening of works by Weber conducted by Sir Roger Norrington. Many players continued to perform in Norrington's London Classical Players and enjoyed his zany, energetic style: 'Roger had this engaging way of putting a cranky idea, a picture in words, into people's heads and creating something entirely new,' says Annette Isserlis. Norrington himself, unlike

Chi-chi Nwanoku MBE.

HAYDN'S 'CREATION' WITH SIR CHARLES MACKERRAS 1989
CHI-CHI NWANOKU MBE (PRINCIPAL DOUBLE BASS)

This was one of those OAE projects that epitomised a sense of occasion and magical discovery. Interestingly, though I had heard and played *The Creation* before, it had not taken hold of me in the way that it did this time. I soon realised that what made it feel so unique and special was down to the fact that every one of us involved were responsible for making this happen. This orchestra was our creation, and we were there to nourish, teach it and help it grow. So, like proud parents, we were unconditionally nurturing it to its full potential. There was that unspoken glow between us, as in any family, where every member had their unique role in how we created our 'Creation'.

This was only our second or third project with Mackerras and to me symbolic in that it seemed synonymous with what the OAE was setting out to do.

This is music that really speaks and tells a story with honesty, warmth, tenderness, innocence, humour, passion, pain and power. No programmatic piece of music had yet reached into my guts quite as literally as this particular experience.

I had the added advantage of playing 'continuo' and Sir Charles had me at the front, right under his nose, next to the fortepiano (a novel place for me to sit then). He was masterful in the way he nurtured us through the rehearsals and really got us to 'create' every plant, creature and atmosphere invented. He seated the cello and bass sections either side of the Orchestra, which was particularly effective in the creation of the whales! The deep surging bass line simply wrapped itself around the Orchestra. Sitting at the front, away from my section in that movement had me feeling rather like a baby whale swimming somewhere in the middle, upstream of my family!

The most touching memories for me, though, are of 'Sunrise', where Sir Charles held and suspended the tension and moment of release in our dynamics, as the incredible harmonic progression unfolded until the actual second when the sun bursts into the sky; the other was how he enabled us to portray the innocence of the stars coming out for their first time. I thought I could practically SEE them!

All of this was possible because we were ready, receptive and hungry to take our interpretations unanimously to the highest level possible, in an environment where everyone's 'voice' counted.

Sir Charles Mackerras: 'Playing a period instrument is like driving a car and having to double de-clutch, the handicaps one suffers are tremendous... but I never wondered for a moment whether it was worth it: it was an inspiration.'

some others, had little interest in running his own permanent orchestra and had even encouraged the players to take on his LCP and run it themselves: 'I thoroughly approved of their enterprise,' he explains. ' I said to Felix, "If I'd known you were going to set up an orchestra, you could have had mine!" The only reason I had my orchestra was so that I had a musical laboratory for my experiments, it was never a career vehicle for me. I said they could take it over, but I do understand that it was important psychologically for them to set something up on their own.' (Ultimately, nearly a decade later, the OAE did absorb the work of the LCP).

Norrington's first concert was a celebration of Weber's bi-centenary, a remarkably long and ambitious programme with impressive soloists: Antony Pay starred in the Clarinet Concerto no. 1, Melvyn Tan in the Konzertstück in F minor and Elizabeth Connell sang two opera arias. It did not escape the slowest of critics that this was not exactly repertoire from the Age of Enlightenment. But this mattered not a jot when 'one heard the (valveless) horns from Elfland blowing at the start of the *Oberon* and *Der Freischütz* overtures, it really did seem the dawn of a new epoch in orchestral music.' wrote Meiron Bowen in *The Guardian*.

The wind parts, released from the thick, homogenised 20th Century string sound, came through each with its distinctive tang. The two concertos 'showed just how far from the squawk, squeak and rattle era of authentic performance we have moved,' continued Bowen. Antony Pay remembers Simon Rattle coming to a rehearsal – 'He was fascinated. I think it was after hearing that rehearsal that he decided to become involved.' Rattle agrees: 'It was a step on the way.'

Another conductor who received an invitation in 1987 was the Dutch harpsichordist and director Gustav Leonhardt, revered for his pioneering recordings of Bach Cantatas with Nikolaus Harnoncourt. Susan Sheppard played continuo cello for him: 'I always felt he was an invaluable link to the Baroque music revival in its first form, in the Sixties. He has a phenomenal knowledge and experience of Bach, perhaps more than anyone else in the world, and there was an integrity about his approach I loved. He had very simple basic ideals. He wanted the first beat to sound and the other beats to be so, so light. I think the recordings of the secular Cantatas we did with him for Philips are some of our best. He was always unfailingly polite and his command of English vocabulary was greater than we could ever aspire to. In some ways he lives the life of someone from the 17th Century, wearing the same clothes each day, living in a national monument with no heating, his single-minded devotion to his art – it all fits but for this peculiar quirk: his passion for fast cars. He test-drives Ferraris in Modena, and owns an Aston Martin.'

A MAN OF EXPERIENCE

Sir Charles Mackerras was in many ways an obvious choice of conductor: not only was he a consummate 'modern' professional but he had, for over forty years, been an energetic scholar of Classical scores, a force in the revival of Handel opera and he had even conducted Rameau opera for Lina Lalandi at Covent Garden and in Athens. It was Mackerras, after all, who made the first recording in 1959 of Handel's *Music for the Royal Fireworks* with the original line-up of instruments, but he had never until then been associated with the up-and-coming Early Music scene. His first OAE concert in 1987 included the Overture to *Don Giovanni*, Mozart's 'Linz' Symphony and the 'Haffner' Serenade. He remembers the first re-

Top: Oboist Anthony Robson preparing a new reed while on tour in Rome. Below: Charles Fullbrook tuning the timpani for a concert conducted by Nicholas Kraemer.

hearsal vividly: 'Monica Huggett was leading, and I had a certain amount of difficulty in getting her to come and discuss the bowings. She said, "Why are you worrying about bowings, they didn't write in bowings in the 18th Century!". I liked to have everything meticulously marked in, but she was right – they didn't do that in the 18th Century. The fact was I was used to so few rehearsals, I couldn't waste a minute of time. With hindsight, I can see her point, because they really did have many more rehearsals than any symphony orchestra. They were encountering repertoire for the first time on period instruments, so they needed to work very hard on it.'

Mackerras was always sympathetic to the fact that the musicians had technical hurdles to overcome: 'Playing a period instrument is like driving a car and having to double de-clutch. The handicaps that one suffers with those wind instruments are tremendous. Instruments were built so your fingers could go over the holes, but the holes were not necessarily in the best place for 'just' intonation. Playing the horn and making those chromatic notes with your fist, trying to get the tone consistent, is incredibly hard – the horn players have to work so much harder to get it in tune, although Andrew Clark and Roger Montgomery and all the other OAE horn players do it extremely well. And gut strings are unstable, they do go out of tune very quickly.'

Rehearsing in the Sheldonian Theatre, Oxford: the OAE were immediately 'known as the crack band in London' according to Simon Foster of Virgin Classics.

Was he ever frustrated by these technical hurdles? 'I never wondered for a moment whether it was worth it: it was an inspiration. To be able to hear the phrasing, the sounds – the fact that the notes decay so much more rapidly, it opens up the texture. And it also answers a whole lot of questions: like the overture to *Don Giovanni* – the minim in the bass and the crotchet in the top, they are quite similar because of the way the sound decays, in modern times people mistakenly sustain it through the bar. It's taught me a tremendous amount.'

A DEAL WITH VIRGIN

Hard on the heels of Mackerras's first concerts came his first recording with The Age of Enlightenment: Schubert's 9th Symphony released on the newly-formed Virgin Classics label. Simon Foster, who had been working at EMI, was asked by Richard Branson to set up the label in 1987. 'I was already an enthusiast for this repertoire, and the OAE were known to be the crack band in London – it was an obvious connection with our new label. Judith Hendershott made the introduction: she was very effective at driving the relationship.' But there were problems: lack of a figurehead being one. 'It had its disadvantages in terms of building an identity. But it also meant we could bring different conductors to the recordings, it gave flexibility. The Haydn 'Paris' Symphonies with Kuijken were fantastic as were Gustav Leonhardt's CPE Bach symphonies and concertos. Conductors normally want to do symphonies rather than chamber pieces or concertos, while with this orchestra you had these sensational soloists all coming forward, bursting with ideas. I would say 80% of their suggestions I took up, which is rare. They were such an intelligent lot. I have particularly fond memories of the Bach concerto discs including the Violin and Oboe concertos with Anthony Robson, Alison Bury and Elizabeth Wallfisch.'

Sometimes the democratic nature of the OAE delayed decision-making, according to Simon Foster: 'I do remember there were five-hour ADC meetings, every aspect of a recording had to be carefully weighed before the committee. Sometimes opportunities were fudged or lost because of it. I must say I wore out a lot of shoe leather tramping about London trying to track people down to get agreement!'

The Virgin relationship resulted in 14 recordings over the next decade, although when Simon Foster left in 1992 and Virgin was taken over by EMI the plans were curtailed. 'Virgin became a French label,' explains Foster, 'and economics were becoming tight. Each recording had to be costed separately as recordings were not written into a player's contract as they would have been in a salaried orchestra. When the recession hit in 1989, sponsorship of recordings plummeted and it was very hard to fund the more ambitious recordings.'

IDOMENEO

To return to 1987, the newly-fledged Orchestra was about to announce their most ambitious project yet: a concert performance of *Idomeneo* with Simon Rattle in the Queen Elizabeth Hall. Rattle was a name to conjure with even at this early date and the players knew it was important to make a connection. Tim Mason, Antony Pay and Marshall Marcus had played in the National Youth Orchestra with Rattle, while Warnock had been a family friend, and arranged for the student Rattle to conduct a concert at Hertford College in Oxford, where his father was Principal. Rattle's own journey towards period instruments had started many years before: 'For me it starts with David Munrow, at the Royal Academy. Obviously a lot of us worked with him during the little time we had him. He was unbelievably inspirational, but I didn't immediately go in that direction, I had a lot of other things to learn. Eventually I became very frustrated by the way that modern orchestras played Classical music – it was very confused. My great moment came when Bernard Haitink asked me to conduct *Idomeneo* at Glyndebourne. I hadn't been able to make head nor tail of it, and Bernard said in his gruff, Dutch way – "Go and listen to Harnoncourt's recording, I think you'll like it." That was the start of my journey, my realisation that the music seemed grateful to be played in this way, that this made sense of the score. I went to Micaela Comberti to study Baroque bowing. It wasn't just a

Sir Simon Rattle

IDOMENEO, QEH, 1987, SIMON RATTLE

I knew we had to do it. We needed a colossal number of rehearsals – about 20, I think. We all needed that, because they had no shared habits of how to play this opera together as a group. And few had tackled an opera of that length before. It was an unforgettable time. In many ways it changed my life. We could really help each other: I learnt an enormous amount from them, and they needed someone who could make them into an orchestra. At that time, and for some time after that, they would use me as a conductor when they needed me, and then exclude me. That was because they were used to not relying on a conductor, a technical, physical conductor. David Munrow was a good physical conductor as well as an extraordinary musician, but that has not always been the case in Early Music – some of these pioneering musicians were foremostly instrumentalists and lacked a basic technique. But in some ways I think I've changed, though, and maybe some of that way of conducting was imprisoning. The OAE has made me a lot freer – they think so much in shapes and phrases, they are interested in the content rather than the style, what does it *mean,* not what is right? That's why it is so deeply satisfying to work with them.

case of buying a new set of clothes, one had to learn a new way of thinking.'

Rattle remembers a key conversation he had with Tim Mason when he conducted a pick-up orchestra for a CND charity concert organised by Mason: 'We played Mozart and he said to me, "Everything you are asking for is what we are trying to do. Why don't you come and work with these instruments?". And I realised I was starting to meet old friends again, like Tim, like Libby Wallfisch, who I had accompanied at the Academy, and it became something necessary, that I must do. I was already working with the City of Birmingham Symphony Orchestra (CBSO) on everything that I was learning. Still, I was staggered when Tim and Felix actually came to me and said "Will you do it?".

His response to the invitation was characteristically decisive, according to Warnock: "I've got to do *Idomeneo*!" he declared. 'We had absolutely no experience of promoting such an event with an international cast, but we knew it *had* to happen.' Hendershott managed to secure the first-class cast Rattle had chosen: including Arleen Auger, Philip Langridge and Carol Vaness as Elektra. But as the time drew near, it became clear there was a huge shortfall in the funding. Says Warnock: 'The overdraft from the bank was running out. I remember us sitting in a Board meeting and saying we would have to cancel it if no more money could be found in a week.'

It was at this crisis point that the Board rallied and showed leadership. A key feature of the OAE Board over the years has been the extraordinary degree of trust that its members have placed in the musicians' intuition about what is artistically important, supported by an actively practical approach to solving problems. Players and non-players alike have worked shoulder to shoulder in a rare atmosphere of harmony. To return to 1987, Christopher Lawrence suggested they might like to meet his friend Martin Smith. Smith had been highly successful in Citibank and Bankers Trust, and had recently started up his own corporate finance investment banking business Phoenix Securities. 'I had never supported an arts organisation before,' recalls Smith, 'but I thought Phoenix is new, we are entrepreneurial, we are a band of refugees from the big corporations, and this funny-sounding orchestra is new and entrepreneurial and another sort of group of refugees.' He asked to meet some of the players: Marcus remembers himself, Judith and Tim being paraded before the trademark Smith bow-tie on the 25th floor of the Hong-Kong and Shanghai Building. Smith was impressed: 'As soon as I heard them speak, I thought they were very interesting people and seemed to know exactly what they were doing. But as we went through the numbers I began to think, "They haven't a clue" – this had all the prospects of turning into a complete disaster. They were at least £20k short. I said "How are you going to get through this project without going bust?" and Tim Mason replied, "We thought you might have some bright ideas about that!"'

Smith did, indeed, have a bright idea. He contacted John Gunn and Peter Goldie, at British and Commonwealth, knowing Gunn was passionate about Mozart. Gunn was intrigued, and quickly agreed: a cheque for £20k duly arrived. 'That sort of thing so rarely works out so simply, but thank God it did,' says Smith. From that moment on, he committed himself to supporting the Orchestra and has done so ever since. The players couldn't believe their luck: it is hard to imagine now what might have happened had those two performances of *Idomeneo* not taken place, since they proved critical to the OAE's future success.

Martin Smith: 'As soon as I heard them speak, I thought they were very interesting people and seemed to know exactly what they were doing.'

View of the audience from the old theatre at Glyndebourne.

A NEW DAWN AT GLYNDEBOURNE

Few have forgotten those performances. Chi-chi Nwanoku was playing: 'I remember Carol Vaness's bright red skirt, even the hem was all ripped. She was Elektra, she burst on to the stage in this wild way, challenging everyone. She electrified that room, singing from every pore of her body; we had a standing ovation.' They had come a long way: players remember the very first rehearsals were a struggle: Rattle demanded far more flexibility in tempo and expressiveness than they had been used to, and ensemble was initially ragged. But by the time of the performance, the Orchestra's accomplishment wowed the audience: 'The playing was so good,' remarked Rodney Milnes, 'that the OAE didn't sound like a period orchestra... there was a body and incisiveness one misses in second-rate groups, yet also fleetness and flexibility one might miss in modern bands. The oboe screams with pain in 'O voto tremendo', the trombones rasping with majestic menace.'

There was a buzz to the event, keenly felt by members of Glyndebourne's management in the audience. Rattle takes up the story: 'I got it into my head that Peter Hall had to come and hear this. He was instrumental to the OAE coming to Glyndebourne – many people have taken credit but it was really he who pushed it through. He became so excited. He said, "We have to do this!", he had a Messianic zeal.'

Rattle must also take credit, since he was at the time being wooed by Glyndebourne as a successor to Haitink. It was becoming clear that his commitment to the CBSO and his reservations about Glyndebourne's exclusivity would prevent him accepting this. Yet he still exerted an extraordinary influence and when he insisted he would not do the whole Da Ponte trilogy without the OAE, the management knew he meant business. The 1987 *Idomeneo* set the seal on Glyndebourne's agreement: they would start with *Figaro* in 1989. George Christie was quoted as saying they 'jumped in with both feet and without any shadow of reluctance' but members of Glyndebourne's music staff held back, as Rattle recalls: 'The people working with me, the singers, the management, people like Anthony Whitworth-Jones, were enormously supportive. They felt it was a big leap forward. It was the music staff who resisted: they feared that we were going to destroy their Mozart performing tradition – I said "I don't think we're good enough to do that!". And, look, here we are, Mozart survived.'

Commentator Norman Lebrecht tried to stir things up in *The Sunday Times*, talking about 'Figaro-in-the-raw' and the 'summary displacement of the London Philharmonic'. It was a bold move for Glyndebourne, but, with hindsight, a vital one: the subsequent, ground-breaking Handel productions are simply unimaginable without a period orchestra now.

Only a year after its formation, the stage was set for what was now the *Orchestra* of the Age of Enlightenment to become part of Britain's musical establishment. It was the first period instrument orchestra to gain a foothold in an opera house, and Glyndebourne was the first British opera house to hire such an orchestra. Rattle had made a key contribution and there was no going back: 'We were on the map,' says Warnock, 'Glyndebourne meant an income, some dates in the diary. At that point we had to start planning ahead properly; it stopped being a concert by concert operation.' In less than two years, the players had already discovered just what they had set out to find: experience and variety far beyond the confines of the Early Music world.

Taking on the Establishment: 1988-1996

Bassoonist Felix Warnock took over as manager in 1988, his sights set on the creation of a regular London season at the South Bank Centre and, after important concert series including those on Haydn and Bach, the association was formalised in 1993 with an official residency. Relationships with Frans Brüggen, Iván Fischer and Simon Rattle blossomed during this period, Rattle completing the Mozart trilogy with *Don Giovanni* in Glyndebourne's new theatre and taking the Orchestra on its first major European tour in 1994. Mark Elder initiated his exploration of Romantic opera, with a concert performance of Rossini's *Ermione,* followed by Weber's *Euryanthe.* David Pickard took over as manager in 1993, while founding father and Chairman of the Orchestra, cellist Tim Mason, was forced to resign through illness in 1996. Peter Sellars' production of Handel's oratorio *Theodora* was a controversial hit that same year.

1988 Frans Brüggen's first concert at the Sheldonian Theatre, Oxford.

1989 Iván Fischer conducts Haydn Masses at the Queen Elizabeth Hall.

1991 Philippa Brownsword, from the London Classical Players, becomes Orchestra Manager.

1991 *Così fan tutte* at Glyndebourne's old theatre, directed by Trevor Nunn, here in its 1992 revival with Bruno Weil.

Photos: Susan Benn, Mike Hoban

1992 Margaret Faultless, now one of the four leaders, at work.

1993 David Pickard takes over as General Manager.

1994 Janet Reeve, the OAE's first Development Manager, at work finding sponsorship.

1994 Simon Rattle comes off stage in Graz during the first European Tour.

1994 A view of Vienna from the coach: the tour goes on...

1994 Glyndebourne's new Opera House, where the OAE performed *Don Giovanni* for its opening season.

1994 Mark Elder conducts Rossini's *Ermione* at the Queen Elizabeth Hall.

1994 UK Bach tour led by Elizabeth Wallfisch.

1996 Lorraine Hunt Lieberson as Irene in Handel's *Theodora* at Glyndebourne.

Taking on the Establishment

A BOND WITH THE SOUTH BANK

By the end of 1987 the OAE had established itself at Glyndebourne, had a record label contract and was negotiating some major projects at the South Bank Centre. 'It was hard to keep up with the pace of development,' recalls Felix Warnock. In 1988 differences of opinion led to Judith Hendershott's departure. She went on to work at the Lufthansa Festival, and to manage Hausmusik, a chamber group specialising in the early Romantic repertoire and that included several OAE players. Various candidates for a General Manager were interviewed. Felix and the other Board members were not enthused by any of them: 'I remember going to the pub afterwards and rashly saying, "I don't like any of these people – they don't really understand the origins of the Orchestra, what the players want. I could do a better job." I had no wish to give up playing the bassoon, but I could see that now we had started something, we needed to ensure it fulfilled its potential.'

Warnock was duly interviewed and appointed. He had no experience in management at all, but a sure sense of where the Orchestra's trajectory should be heading. He was, more importantly, liked and trusted by the players and had the goodwill of the profession.

However, his first project was a near disaster. 'One of the first calls I had was from the South Bank Centre saying that our major season of late Haydn Masses, planned for 1989, was going to be cancelled.' William Glock, the pioneering Head of Music at the BBC, then retired, had been consulted on the series and had recommended that the OAE perform. It had been planned as a South Bank Centre promotion but, as budgets were cut, it suddenly seemed over-ambitious. 'I *had* to salvage it: these concerts constituted virtually all our activity for that season. I offered to raise the funds for half the amount, which, with Martin Smith's help, we did, and I insisted they went halves. Looking back I think that marked the beginning of our relationship: they saw that we would fight back, they were forced to take us seriously.' The South Bank were certainly impressed by the OAE's ability to find funding. It was at this time that Martin Smith formed a relationship with Sir Victor Blank at Charterhouse Banking Group, which became the Orchestra's first major corporate sponsor. It was noted in *The Daily Telegraph* that the OAE's 'invariably capacity audiences' were making it an attractive prospect for City benefactors.

Graham Sheffield, who became Head of Music at the South Bank Centre in 1990 in the midst of the Hoffman report into London orchestras, has only good memories of the OAE:

'I arrived the day that the London Philharmonic Orchestra's residency was announced and the Philharmonia was up in arms. It was an extremely volatile situation, with open warfare between the orchestras, so the informal relationship with the OAE came like a breath of fresh air: we actually discussed music, and matters of genuine artistic interest! They gradually became part of the fabric of the place. I would say it was one of the best relationships the South Bank Centre ever forged.'

FISCHER AND BRÜGGEN

To return to 1988, two conductors who would become extremely important to the OAE made their first appearances. One was the Hungarian Iván Fischer, who had worked with Harnoncourt and at Kent Opera, where

Andrew Clark, Principal Horn.

several players had encountered him. He came to conduct Mozart symphonies at the City of London Festival that summer. Fischer was not well-known in the UK at the time, but the players were excited by his original approach, as Catherine Mackintosh articulates: 'All the string players loved him instantly. Sometimes he doesn't understand why we can't get things together, because he's not very clear in a conventional way, and that's harder for the winds. But what I love about him is that he brings his musicianship from a completely different route from other people, he has such interesting ideas about colour, and makes one do completely anarchic things in order to win freedom. I remember the Beethoven Fifth Symphony we did with him (in 1999): after the first phrase, you didn't have the faintest idea what was going on, it was musical chaos, but we gradually understood that he wanted organised musical chaos. You wondered if it was going to fall apart, but of course it didn't. He has that ability to make you sit on the edge of your seat.'

Frans Brüggen rehearsing at the Royal Academy of Music: his 'Eroica' was a revelation.

The second revered figure to appear with the OAE in 1988 was Frans Brüggen, who would go on to become one of their two Principal Guest Conductors and remains an Emeritus Conductor to this day. The Beethoven 'Eroica' Symphony he gave that December remains indelibly printed on the musicians' memories, for some because of its revelatory brilliance, to others for its disturbing sense of a work stripped bare.

'I always wondered how he would conduct,' remembers Annette Isserlis, 'whether it would be as if he was still playing the recorder, and in a way it was: all eyes and eyebrows. But his 'Eroica' was a revelation: as soon as he started I thought, we are going on a long journey here, it wasn't just each movement that he had foreseen, it was the whole symphony, he created a huge arch structure, he paced it, phrased it, as a whole, incredibly well.' Others in the Orchestra were struck by Brüggen's acute ear: 'He could tune the winds with amazing accuracy', recalls viola player Martin Kelly, 'That ability to analyse exactly what he was hearing is very rare, and of course the winds respected him absolutely.' Brüggen also brought his own Orchestra of the 18th Century over and combined the orchestras in a concert. He later compared the two in an interview: 'The musicians in London have to fight for their living and have to rush from one orchestra to another, and that means in order to be asked back to play they feel they should be impeccable, so the attitude becomes one of avoiding risk. It has its advantages, they learn very quickly, and they are very disciplined, whereas our orchestra is a bunch of savages, difficult to handle sometimes, very cheerful and wild and that manifests itself in the playing….' Sadly, the pressures the London musicians work under remain, despite the OAE's best efforts to carve out as much rehearsal time as possible.

THE ROAD LESS TRODDEN

At about that time members of the Board and ADC began asking who was actually playing in the OAE: there were about 140 members able to vote on decisions, but many of these had never played. It was immediately noticed by critics that the OAE's musicians were not exclusively involved in period instrument performance. This seemed to lend credibility to the enterprise, such was the prejudice against Early Music performers at the time: 'such lively, and historically uncategorisable musicians as Antony Pay, Anthony Halstead and double bassist Chi-chi Nwanoku' wrote Hilary Finch in *The Times*, 'solid professionals, better known in modern music' noticed another.

So what did bring these musicians of such disparate experience together? At the time the OAE was formed, many were still performing in modern ensembles, including the Academy of St. Martin in the Fields, the London Mozart Players, the BBC Symphony Orchestra, Endymion Ensemble, the London Sinfonietta and other contemporary music groups, such as Tim Mason's Capricorn, as well as in the period instrument groups. From out of their rich collective musical experience it seems that a shared spirit of enquiry, a curiosity, an engagement with the fundamental questions raised by musical texts drew them together.

Antony Pay had had a long and distinguished career in contemporary music. 'I think I found that after 15 years of being at the cutting edge of contemporary music I wanted to look at other aspects of music than the attempt simply to do something *different*, which seemed to be the concern of so many contemporary composers. The fact that we don't know exactly what the 'normal' style was for Classical and Baroque performers means that we have to think carefully. I liked that musical, intellectual challenge: it was a welcome change of emphasis from the routine of playing the next impossible score.'

The instruments themselves set new challenges for Pay too. 'With as yet untested repertoire, the instruments almost always set us problems that we haven't encountered before – perhaps the same problems faced by our historical counterparts. On the other hand, they sometimes solve problems that we haven't really seen how best to solve on modern instruments.'

This solving of problems was one of the attractions the instruments had to some players. For Chi-chi Nwanoku it was an instinctive sense of rightness: 'I had been taught by my Italian teacher to vibrate on every single

Iván Fischer

IVÁN FISCHER (CONDUCTOR)

All musicians need a certain level of arrogance in order to believe in the way they perform. Of course we all think that ours is the right way to play Bach (or Bartók). Fürtwangler was interested in other aspects of Bach than those we focus on today. Neither is more right than the other. A serious musician is always fascinated in everything that brings him or her closer to the understanding of the composition. Period instruments certainly help a lot in this understanding. But I remember an earlier generation who were excited about Schenker's analysis more than about the sound and character of instruments.

It seems to me that the pride (or arrogance if you wish) of knowing better is now fading. In fact this knowledge has never been much more than a few details of sound, rhythm, articulation and pitch. The OAE has passed this stage. It is a group of musicians who know very well that an authentic performance can be both great and miserable. My impression is that they are more interested in musicianship, talent, original ideas than revealing new things of performance practice.

Comparing the OAE to a symphony orchestra offers very easy, almost clichéd answers. Yes, it can sound more fresh, lighter and more alive. But I think the musician is more important than the instrument. The human qualities, the mentality of an orchestra is the crucial issue, not the instruments being used. And the OAE is a special orchestra because of the high level of motivation, keen interest and devotion. The danger of any orchestra is when they switch off. I have a feeling with the OAE that they are involved with the music all the time.

note. And when I was studying Eccles Sonatas I just knew the music wasn't asking for that. I played with the Academy of St. Martin in the Fields. We played Classical music in a fast, flashy, powerful, exciting style but I knew at the end of the day I didn't feel musically fulfilled, there was a dimension missing, but I found it with the OAE. Now I have embraced that sound concept totally, starting with a clean sound and not messing it up'.

Lisa Beznosiuk discovered the wooden flute while at college: 'At that time flautists usually played with this crazy vibrato, in quite an unnatural way. The sound and character of the Baroque flute made complete sense to me, rather than the high-octane glamorous silver flute on which, I now realised, I had always tried to produce too "pure" a tone. At last it was possible for me to make the sound I had always had in my head, on this simple wooden instrument. And it goes much further than just cutting out vibrato which, in any case, is very much a part of 18th Century music. Phrasing, rhythm, varied articulation and rhetoric are also crucial elements in the performance and it was fantastic to discover that playing on original instruments actually helped me to play the music.'

Lisa Beznosiuk: 'At last it was possible for me to make the sound I had always had in my head, on this simple wooden instrument.'

There was a similar Damascene conversion for some string players: 'I found when I picked up the Baroque bow at college,' recalls Catherine Mackintosh, 'it answered a lot of questions about how to play unaccompanied Bach: it's much easier to articulate with a Baroque bow, there's more light and shade within the bow stroke.' She, like many others, had been inspired by the work of David Munrow and by pioneer Francis Baines, who played in the OAE, and influenced an entire generation through his viola teaching and rich, expressive double bass playing, including Lisa Beznosiuk: 'Many of today's OAE members will remember with fondness Francis's unique and idiosyncratic contribution to the sound and rhythm of a French dance movement or a poignant Prelude through his variety of expressive bow gestures, his enormous Baroque bow looking for all the world as though it could also fire arrows! Francis and June, his violinist wife, generously invited their students to weekly consort sessions at their house in Barnes to play the 5 and 6 part viol repertoire and, as if by magic, would rustle up dinner.'

Principal oboist Anthony Robson had always liked playing the recorder as a student, so was used to cross-fingerings: 'In some ways the oboe is the most awkward instrument in the orchestra, but the timbre of the Baroque oboe is so special, there is a wider range of dynamics, a warmer, softer, more diffuse sound, due to the larger reed. Some modern players would get a lovely surprise if they tried the older oboes: it's physically easier to make a sound, you don't need so much stamina and there are more colours available for lots of the notes. On the down side, you need more technical expertise to finger notes and the tuning is more difficult.'

For other players there were more mundane considerations: Nicholas Logie, returning from some years playing viola in the Vienna Symphony Orchestra, was advised to start playing on gut strings by the inspirational Baroque violinist Micaela Comberti, with whom many had studied. Comberti was a true evangelist, but the bald fact was that taking up the Baroque violin or viola would expand the number of opportunities to work in London.

The prejudice that Baroque players were simply those who weren't good enough to pass an audition for a modern orchestra continued to be touted long after the period instrument world was thoroughly professionalised. Nwanoku can remember her colleagues at the Academy of St. Martin trying to dissuade her from going in that direction: '"Why are you taking a step backwards? Why do you want to join that lot of cranky, tree-hugging, bed-wetters?", they would say.' Gender politics were at work here too: many of the freelance period instrument bands had attracted a female majority, for reasons of their flexibility and the low income that initially drove men away, while the symphony orchestras at the time were still male bastions.

Rattle remembers how in 1989 the OAE was still settling on a core personnel: 'We were getting to know each other, to develop an orchestra, and see who was going to be flexible enough. People had come from so many different backgrounds. There was a lot of argument. At first there was an idea that different sorts of musicians would be used for different repertoire: eventually, they did find a core of players who were sufficiently flexible.'. Principal positions began to be shared by small groups or pairs of people. Roy Goodman, who had led the first concert among others began to spend more time conducting, and a group of women began to share the role: Elizabeth Wallfisch, Catherine Mackintosh and Alison Bury, joined in the early Nineties by Margaret Faultless. All four have also been willing to play in the section, a legacy of the egalitarian principles on which the OAE was set up. Wallfisch eventually left as a regular leader to focus more on directing and solo work, and was made guest leader along with Marieke Blankestijn. Catherine Mackintosh retired as a leader in 2006, but continues to play as a regular violinist in the Orchestra. Only in its 21st birthday season are trials underway for a new leader to replace Mackintosh.

THE DA PONTE TRILOGY AT GLYNDEBOURNE

By the time *Figaro* opened at Glyndebourne in 1989, it was clear this was a virtuoso group of players, but the old theatre did not help their cause. Bayan Northcott in *The Independent* spoke of an orchestral sound that 'travesties Mozart's scoring' and blamed the depth of the pit, a problem they grappled with through two productions. Others questioned the elaborate ornamentation that Rattle had insisted on adding to the vocal lines. But John Rockwell of *The New York Times* made two prescient observations: the first was that such a production of Mozart, 'prepared with care and dis-

Felix Warnock with Frans Brüggen.

FRANS BRÜGGEN'S BEETHOVEN 'EROICA' SYMPHONY, 1988
BY FELIX WARNOCK (BASSOONIST AND GENERAL MANAGER)

Brüggen is a musical giant and he does the most wonderful Beethoven. It was amazingly different from anything we had done with an English conductor, he brought something completely new. It felt as if we were playing new music. When you do this repertoire on a modern bassoon you simply don't come near that, it is relatively easy to play, it really doesn't make major technical demands. When you play it on the instrument that it was written for, it is extremely hard to do, it stretches the instrument almost beyond the limit of its capability, which gives the performance that element of challenge. It's highly risky, but if everything works, it's like playing the work for the first time.

Brüggen captured something of that: it was unforgettable, we were on the edge of our seats. We had been too comfortable, too familiar with conductors in other ensembles. Suddenly here was Brüggen proving exactly what the Orchestra set out to prove: that you would raise the level by bringing in new musical minds.

crimination and according to the musical, stylistic and social assumptions of his time, can be far more contemporary than many more self-conscious and theatrically provocative interpretations.' While scholarly debate raged over whether or not 'authentic' performance was simply modernism in fancy dress, OAE players were glad to acknowledge they were part of an absolutely contemporary movement.

Rockwell's second point about the 1989 *Figaro* was that 'it marks the most dramatic incursion thus far of established conductors – or what instrumentalists like to call 'real' conductors - into the early music arena.' While Harnoncourt had already taken his expertise out to modern symphony orchestras, the OAE was the only period band in the world to welcome a modern conductor in.

The OAE playing under Rattle: it was the first period orchestra in the world to welcome established modern conductors in.

Despite some luke-warm reviews, the players remember the first *Figaro* with great affection. 'After the first *Figaro*, I thought I would be happy to die now, playing that wonderful music at that level,' recalls Lisa Beznosiuk. Librarian and viola player Colin Kitching observes that the length of the Glyndebourne season became an important time for the development of the ensemble: 'Having a regular team doing 16 performances on the trot pays enormous dividends in terms of ensemble: the discipline is so good for the Orchestra and it clarifies capabilities.'

The next instalment of the cycle, the 1991 *Così fan tutte*, in Trevor Nunn's vivacious production, starred Sir Thomas Allen as Alfonso: after the first rehearsal he came up to Simon Rattle with tears in his eyes saying, 'If I had been singing with that orchestra all my life, I would have ten years more of an opera career ahead of me!' It was in the new theatre for *Don Giovanni* in 1994 that the Orchestra really came into its own: the warm and intimate acoustic optimised their range of colours and timbres, in a way that few other venues have ever done. In an interview at the time, Rattle was revelling in the fulfilment of his original plan: 'Period instruments have more colour, flavour, shape and less weight than modern ones. They are more tangy, more *piccante*. It is to do with clarity, enunciation and drama, with pronouncing the notes as you would pronounce words – music as speech. The great thing is we can play full out with the greatest passion and still sound like Mozart.' Those critics who actually heard the Orchestra beneath Warner's provocative production, were transfixed: 'Rattle's conducting is breathtakingly taut and febrile: young man's Mozart this, full of sexual energy and wit, the textures and harmonies thrillingly exposed in the playing of the OAE,' enthused Rupert Christiansen in *The Spectator*. This was the controversial staging in which the Don finally obsesses over a plaster effigy of the Madonna: 'Oh, I remember the tremendous sound of stomping in that production,' recalls Catherine Mackintosh. 'It was all the vicars walking out. I felt like saying, 'If you have a problem with sin, don't come to see Mozart!'

MARK ELDER AND RARE ROMANTIC OPERA

By the time of *Don Giovanni*, the players had also made forays into the world of 19th Century opera with Mark Elder. Elder, another National Youth Orchestra ally, had always been close to the OAE's plans and couldn't wait to start working with this group of colleagues. His first concert was Haydn's *The Seasons* in 1989, and the impact the musicians made on him was instant: 'It was a life-changing experience. It enabled me to experiment with sounds and styles which I had never encountered. I remember being struck by the purity of tone and natural way they phrased. I'd often found performances of this repertoire inflexible, heavy and square, so to conduct it with the OAE was a revelation.

Elder was eager to start performing opera and in 1992 he alighted upon Rossini's *Ermione* for two performances in the Queen Elizabeth Hall. 'The stylistic journey the Orchestra had travelled, from the Baroque, through Classical and Beethoven to Rossini, was vital, It gave a whole different perspective.'

Max Loppert, writing in *The Financial Times*, recognised the significance of the performance: '…an extremely exciting performance, played and sung with biting attack and limpid phrasing… But beyond the individual pleasures, it was the work itself that provided the feeling of revelation: a high-wire mixture, perfectly balanced, of Classical forms and Romantic passions that keeps the drama unfolding at fever pitch.'

Felix Warnock was particularly proud of this success, but both he and Elder were disappointed that when Glyndebourne took up *Ermione* two years later, it was with the LPO rather than the OAE.

Mark Elder's next project, Weber's *Euryanthe* in 1994, part of the Deutsche Romantik series, drew even wider attention. 'Who could have believed it could be so stirring?,' asked David Murray in *The Financial Times*. 'The QEH was packed out with the OAE's devoted audience – but it is a thousand pities that *Euryanthe* is not running for two or three more evenings.' Again, the Orchestra had succeeded in making a case for Weber to an audience of sceptics, placing the composer in his rightful position: 'The

Anthony Robson

THE MARRIAGE OF FIGARO AT GLYNDEBOURNE, SUMMER 1989
ANTHONY ROBSON (PRINCIPAL OBOE)

For me, the OAE's entry into the rarified world of Glyndebourne was the moment when the Orchestra really *arrived*.

There are hazy memories, getting even fuzzier as time passes, aided by a grainy, rapidly perishing, off-TV video (which would be a great testament if commercially released…)

It was a very bold move on the part of Simon Rattle, and indeed a very brave one for Glyndebourne to take the plunge and introduce a period band into such hallowed territory. But it turned out to be an astute one, which over time has proven to have been a wise one and brought huge dividends on all sides.

I had adored *The Marriage of Figaro* from a distance for as long as I can remember, and I'm sure if someone had told me back in my student days at the RAM that one day I would play principal oboe in *Figaro* at Glyndebourne, I would never have believed it.

Images flood back: that small, old theatre with its wonderful sense of intimacy in Mozart; the cramped, baking hot pit (but with a small, inviting artists' bar within steps of the stage door where a quick something to quench your thirst on the way home was 'obligato'); the sheer excitement of being involved in something so pioneering; Simon's sure and inspiring direction on the podium, the beautiful Peter Hall production; and sets to die for by John Bury. I still remember the gasp of admiration and spontaneous applause as the curtain rose on the fourth act and a very special portrayal of the role of Marcellina by Felicity Palmer that one will never experience again. And, finally, that third act sextet. I only have to smell a tobacco plant to be taken back to those magical evenings.

music itself never fails to astonish: you have to keep reminding yourself that it is written in 1823, a mere 30 years after *The Magic Flute*, while much of it sounds like the Wagner of *Tristan*,' noted Barry Millington in *The Times*. David Murray, and others, concluded that Weber had understood the instruments of his own age so perfectly that 'modern playing-machines can never do him more than dusty justice.' 'The Orchestra lost a bucket-load of cash,' recalls Elder. But the gamble paid off when Glyndebourne later decided to stage *Euryanthe* with the OAE.

Violinist and leader Alison Bury: 'I remember the expression on Mark Elder's face when something sounded really dreadful – a look of utter disbelief, despair. But he rehearses so thoroughly, we always came through.'

Elder was now impatient to work with the Orchestra on early Verdi, and in quick succession *Simon Boccanegra* (1995) and *Alzira* (1996) were performed. 'When we did *Simon Boccanegra* in its first version it really inspired the management at Covent Garden. They could see the impact it would make. I remember talking to Nicholas Payne about bringing the OAE into the pit at Covent Garden for the Verdi festival. It was a great shame that the festival did not reach its completion.' That same year he conducted the OAE in a disc of Bellini arias with Jane Eaglen. 'You have to remember, it took two or three rehearsals before it started to sound any good at all in those days – it was a major job bringing them together as an orchestra.' Violinist Alison Bury well remembers the expression on Elder's face 'when something sounded really dreadful - it was a look of utter disbelief, despair. But he rehearses so thoroughly, we always came through.' Elder was rewarded with complete concentration: 'They would engage absolutely with these scores, they were determined to achieve that unity and solidity. I remember when we were doing *Linda de Chamonix* it only happened at the last minute, but they got there, and it's on a BBC tape.'

A STRANGER IN THEIR MIDST

In 1993 a slight young man who had worked at Kent Opera was appointed manager, to work alongside Warnock, who became Artistic Administrator, until he left to manage The English Concert at the end of 1994. His name was David Pickard. He was the first OAE manager ever to come from outside the core musical family, and the first to have had no connections in the Early Music world: 'I came from an interesting standpoint: as a music student at Cambridge I used to go away and listen to Korngold and Richard Strauss to get away from these insufferable people who told me that there was only Baroque music and it could only be heard on period instruments. "Authenticity" among some musicians seemed to have become a religious cult which excluded all other forms of musical expression and had a total disdain for great musicians of the past. When I got to the OAE I discovered an organisation engaged in something incredibly new, exciting and different: I then realised that what drew people towards that orchestra was a desire to not be run of the mill, to explore, to be challenged. None of them had taken the easy route of joining a salaried symphony orchestra. They had all taken the rockier path, had done research, freelanced in Baroque and contemporary orchestras; there was a real enquiring spirit at work.'

Pickard had never run an orchestra before, but was a good listener. 'He was an iron fist in a velvet glove, in a way,' comments Martin Smith, 'He was willing to listen, to ask the right questions.' Felix Warnock's vigorous planning had resulted in a huge increase in activity, and that very season saw the start of the OAE's official residency at the South Bank Centre. The SBC had plans for seven or eight OAE concerts a year, there was to be an increased involvement with the opening of the new theatre at Glyndebourne, and there was the first major European tour with Rattle on the horizon (spring of 1994). The Orchestra was about to take off: it had gone from giving a series of *ad hoc* concerts to having a year-round impact in London and a regular presence in Europe. 'It was an exciting time,' recalls Pickard, 'but it brought with it serious issues of funding.'

After his early coup, Martin Smith became the Orchestra's chief bread-winner for its first ten years. He had introduced Charterhouse, and Goldman Sachs, which not only sponsored Rattle's big European tours, but even provided a private aircraft for it. However, he was understandably keen that a broader base of funding be established. The appointment of Janet Reeve as the first Development Manager resulted in a more diverse funding portfolio: the reliance on corporate donors had become too great and she, with assistance from Martin's wife, Elise Becket Smith, initiated a Friends scheme and Chair Patrons scheme which has become a model of its kind. Later, Benefactors were also introduced. Says David, 'It has proved to be the way forward for most arts organisations. When you find people who do have a genuine personal interest in the music and what you are trying to do, they tend to be very loyal and our supporters quickly became part of the OAE family.'

What particularly impressed Pickard was the players' attitude to funding. 'I had come from Kent Opera which had 50% of its funding from the Arts Council. When that funding was removed it went into liquidation. It's as simple as that. It was a very unhappy six months to see that wonderful company, with the vision that it had, being hijacked by cuts. The OAE had a very different approach: here was a group coming up with a fantastic vision for a project or a concert, and sitting down and trying to work out how it could be financed. The players instinctively knew what the financial equation was. That was tremendously liberating: of course the targets were challenging, but there wasn't the us and them division. They would come and willingly talk to sponsors after concerts, they would engage in the whole process.'

Mark Elder

ERMIONE BY ROSSINI, QEH, 1992, MARK ELDER (CONDUCTOR)

The influence of the OAE has been enormous; they were prepared to extend the 19th Century repertoire, particularly operatic repertoire, to be played on period instruments, to take a creative approach. The players are so well-informed and so interested to find out more. Rossini's *Ermione* was pivotal in all this. Rossini's dates are actually so close to Beethoven's, though no one speaks of them in the same breath. I felt we could apply the things we had learnt about performing Beethoven to a Rossini opera. Rossini's music matters to me profoundly, and this repertoire is so very dependent on the right interpretation, it can die in the wrong hands. Most books on Rossini's operas don't give *Ermione* the time of day. I listened to a tape with a modern symphony orchestra and was hooked. I had to try and communicate my excitement to the Orchestra, and at that stage we were still fairly new to each other, so it was a real voyage of discovery. Those light, flexible, articulating bows were perfect; the brass lent a brightness without heaviness. The performance seemed to burst through the walls of the QEH, it was so powerful. We had two tenors, Bruce Ford and Keith Lewis, who could do justice to these amazingly difficult parts and it was the first time the wonderful Anna-Caterina Antonacci had sung in London. Everybody who was there – and it was packed - was enveloped in our experiment.

CLIMBING MOUNT EVEREST

The Artistic Direction Committee (ADC), elected by players, was the keystone of the organisation, but its operation was never straightforward. Warnock remembers it being on the 'first diagram' that Tim Mason had drawn up for the Orchestra's structure. 'It was necessary but uncomfortable. Players would come up with brilliant ideas for concerts and projects, and would wonder why they never seemed to happen, or why, when four years later an idea did come to fruition it was almost unrecognisable. That is in the nature of planning and matching ideals to the practical realities: the process of knitting together a saleable idea in consultation with venues, festivals, promoters, soloists, conductors and agents was more complicated than they at first realised.'

Simon Rattle, Marshall Marcus and Antony Pay at Berlin airport.

One of Pickard's first tasks was to reduce the size of the membership – from approximately 140 to 80 – since players who had never performed with the Orchestra were able to vote on significant aspects of its work. He introduced an annual membership fee, and then streamlined the ADC, from eight to four players, with an annual election. 'I felt I needed to make sure that the elected players realised they were there to represent the other players, not to push their own agendas. It was very important that as many players as possible came and experienced the realities of management. There will always be people who sit at the back of the coach and complain!'

As the number of concerts increased, the ADC could not initiate each one, and eventually a separate Programming Committee was formed to relieve some of the burden. But the fundamental principle remained that the players had the right of veto over whom they worked with and over the direction of major projects. In 1993, when Pickard arrived, Tim Mason, as Chairman of the Board, advised him to seek to put on concerts that would be the artistic highlights of the players' careers. 'I never felt that I was there to fill a diary, which was inspiring. However, as time went on and the players' other freelance work became eroded, this did begin to change, and we planned more dates.' (There were four concerts in 1986; by 2000 there were 73.)

The Orchestra was always famous for its 'Islington democracy', as one promoter termed it, and the strongly independent, original ethos it created. 'Of course, there was a joke that every decision needed a committee,' says Pickard, 'But when an arts organisation is in its start-up phase you do need committees. As it evolves the processes can be simplified.' Pickard saw his role as a balancing job, with Felix Warnock and then James Ellis, from 1997, working as Artistic Administrator on the realisation of the ADC's ideas.

'Trying to make the ADC work and keep everyone happy is like trying to climb Mount Everest,' remarks Marshall Marcus. The most painful aspect of the committee was always its role in personnel: discussions were dogged by status anxiety and territorial loyalties. 'It was at those times that you almost wished for a Neville Marriner or a John Eliot Gardiner to come in and be ruthless,' explains one player. In fact, most recognised such a *volte face* would spell the end of the Orchestra. Bassist Cecilia Bruggemeyer, currently on the ADC, remarks, 'The personnel side is very hard, but it is just one aspect of all the work of the ADC. I think it's worth that tough bit to be able to steer the artistic course of the Orchestra.'

INTERNATIONAL RELATIONS

The opera relationship with Simon Rattle was leading naturally into more symphonic repertoire and in February 1994, the OAE set out with the conductor on a major tour of Europe which culminated at Birmingham's Symphony Hall. The programmes included Haydn's Symphony no. 90, Mozart's Symphony no. 40, Beethoven's Symphony no. 6 and Schubert's Symphony no. 9. Unsurprisingly, it was a sell-out. The Orchestra had already performed in several European countries, most frequently in Spain, but this was the most ambitious plan to date. Some years before, during the planning, Warnock had been pondering the question of the OAE's identity, and wondered if it might not be an advantage to have a public association with two different 'guest' conductors, Rattle and Brüggen, 'to express our double aspirations'. 'This was, of course, against the original principles of the Orchestra, but it helped to communicate the range and versatility, not to say quality, of its work. Simon agreed to it while crossing Marylebone Road with me, which, as you can imagine, can take some time… It must have been to the considerable unease of his management, who had much higher ambitions for him in Berlin and Vienna, and regarded us as a bunch of amateurs at the time. But Simon had faith: what he did for us was very clear, very focused and very helpful. He didn't waver, he didn't think about the next career move, he just said, "Let's see what we can work out."

Returning to opera, 1996 turned out to be a watershed year for the OAE's relationship with Glyndebourne: with hindsight, Peter Sellars' contemporary production of Handel's oratorio *Theodora* was an historic milestone. Those involved in the first performances recognised it as a life-changing experience, but it challenged critics and audiences, and its initial reception was surprisingly reserved. By the time of the revival in 2003 it had reached legendary status. David Pickard recalls reservations among the players about the choice of Peter Sellars to direct this oratorio, but any doubts were soon swept aside by the man himself: 'The players love to hear the director's thoughts on the production, and Sellars was delighted to talk to them: he expressed in very emotional terms what he felt each aria represented, and they were persuaded by his imaginative vision.'

The critics questioned how Sellars' modern American scenario could possibly fit with the OAE under William Christie in the pit: in fact, paradoxically, it was an impressively integrated performance, as Pickard explains: 'I think the fact that the oratorio had not been staged before, that there was no performing tradition, meant that one could look at the work in a completely new way. That sense of newness was so exciting, and the OAE were also coming to it fresh.' Players and critics agreed that William Christie exerted a discipline on the Orchestra that helped bring out the Orchestra's natural sense of colour and made the music really fizz. There were grumbles about Sellars' trademark storm-troopers and the lethal injection scene raised eyebrows, but it was the emotional engagement of the singers that impressed and affected the instrumentalists: 'I'll never forget Lorraine Hunt Lieberson as Irene singing 'Prosperity!' out to that Glyndebourne audience, she was taunting them, holding out the jewels, asking what it was all for,' says violinist Catherine Ford. Lisa Milne, who understudied Dawn Upshaw, was also struck by the scene: 'The audience response was palpable: there was a tension, a shame. It made people feel uncomfortable, and so it should have.'

The OAE later recorded a superlative Handel arias disc with the late Lorraine Hunt Lieberson: 'I was so impressed by the way she took on the arias during the recording, with the same emotional commitment she had shown on stage,' says violinist Alison Bury. It remains a poignant legacy of the OAE's work with Hunt Lieberson, who suffered a recurrence of cancer and died in 2006.

LOSS OF A FOUNDING MEMBER

It was during 1996 that, to the shock and sadness of the Orchestra, the co-principal cellist and Chairman Tim Mason also succumbed to cancer. He died in 1997, aged only 48. Tim had not only been the Orchestra's sole Chairman, but had been relied upon as the conscience of the organisation and a unique source of ideas and innovation. Simon Rattle pays tribute: 'Tim was the heart-beat of the OAE – it was the embodiment of his desire to be freer than he could ever be. He was at the top in terms of musical and philosophical understanding. His mixture of humour, stubbornness and bloody-mindedness was inimitable. He was quite a tightly wound person who wished to be relaxed – and he could understand that something like this orchestra could open out and take risks. Every artistic group needs someone like that. When he died the Orchestra took on a little of that spirit. He was like the booster rocket that helped propel them upwards, he forced them into independence. I shall always be eternally grateful to him – he changed many of our lives.'

As the only remaining musician of the original gang of three still active in the Orchestra, Marshall Marcus was the natural successor as Chairman.

Right: Principal Double Bass Chi-chi Nwanoku MBE.

TIM MASON, CO-PRINCIPAL CELLIST AND CHAIRMAN OF THE ORCHESTRA 1986-1996, BY ANTONY PAY

Though he was totally unpompous, Tim Mason was a serious man. I loved that when you were with him, he took you seriously; and that he would often want to talk with you about his own serious interests, including the OAE, to which he was highly committed.

It was obvious that he was serious about music itself. His collection of performances of all sorts, taped from radio broadcasts, ran into the hundreds, and he had a comprehensive knowledge of the standard orchestral and chamber repertoire, relevant bits of which he liked to produce on his cello, deftly sketching in the harmonies. His own playing coupled precision of intonation with a stylish clarity of expression; I would say that these were also the qualities he rightly looked to the OAE to demonstrate.

His habit of throwing himself into whatever he did showed itself in other ways. He had a surprising talent for being amusingly silly. And you knew that if you travelled to a rehearsal with him, you risked being 'only just not late', because he found it so hard to drag himself away from what he was currently engaged in. 'There's just so much to do!' he complained to me once in the early days, as he and I bucketed along in Jan's old Mini.

Not that he was disorganised. He knew more about loading a dishwasher than anyone. And if he as Chairman visited the OAE office, you could be sure that anything stuck in the works would begin to get unstuck.

Fundamentally, Tim set us an example. He was a deeply thoughtful, deeply trustworthy Chairman of the OAE, and a very good friend. We all miss his reassuring laugh - and his wonderful smile.

Tim Mason

More like Grown-ups: 1997-2002

The Orchestra began working with an increasing variety of different conductors and soloists, including Paavo Järvi, Marin Alsop, Andrew Davis and Vladimir Jurowski, and Viktoria Mullova, Andreas Scholl and Robert Levin. Photographer Eric Richmond was commissioned to photograph the Orchestra, and OAE marketing campaigns became celebrated and much-imitated by other London orchestras. The OAE gathered together a host of world-class conductors for its complete Beethoven symphony cycle in 1999, and fulfilled a long-held dream of many players with its performance of Rameau's *Les Boréades* at the Salzburg Festival that same year under Rattle. Jupiter Asset Management Limited signed a major sponsorship deal in the late Nineties, and the Arts Council provided regular funding for the first time for UK tours, securing the OAE's relationship with St. George's Brandon Hill, in Bristol. In 2001 David Pickard took up the reigns as General Director at Glyndebourne and the OAE's Development Director, Kirsty MacDonald, replaced him.

1997 Counter-tenor Andreas Scholl sings Handel, on a tour with Nicholas McGegan.

1997 Paavo Järvi conducts the OAE in Saint-Saëns and Fauré.

1997 New marketing campaign commissioned by design agency Oxygen, and shot by Eric Richmond.

1997 Poster for the European tour sponsored by Goldman Sachs.

1998 Rattle conducts Berlioz's *La mort de Cléopâtre* in Brussels.

1998 Education takes on an increasingly important role in the work of the players.

1998 *Rodelinda* at Glyndebourne.

1998 Start of a new relationship with St. George's, Brandon Hill.

1999 Robert Levin's first concert with the OAE, performing Mozart .

1999 The complete Beethoven symphony cycle at the South Bank Centre.

2000 Viktoria Mullova's first tour performing Mozart Violin Concertos.

2001 First concert with Vladimir Jurowski , who chose to conduct Glinka and Borodin.

2001 *Fidelio* at Glyndebourne.

2001 Mirror, mirror: new campaign by Eric Richmond; bassoonist Andrew Watts goes back in time.

More like Grown-ups

After David Pickard's arrival, the number of different soloists and conductors working with the OAE increased considerably. Period specialists like Monica Huggett, Anner Bylsma, Melvyn Tan and Ronald Brautigam had always featured in their programmes, but one Classical keyboard specialist who alighted in their midst in 1999 and seemed instantly at home was the American Robert Levin: 'The combination of chamber music and a concerto was wonderful, as it allowed me to enjoy the personalities of the OAE's élite wind players,' recalls Levin. His infectious wit and spontaneity proved an inspiration to the OAE and their audience. 'Robert has it all,' remarks Marshall Marcus. 'In equal parts scholar, performer and improviser, an ideal Enlightenment musician.' He has since joined the Orchestra in Mendelssohn, Beethoven, Haydn, Schumann and Forster, and relishes the relationship: 'I have a sense in every performance that my ideas find an extraordinary response from the OAE that is invigorating and inspiring.'

Just as the Orchestra wanted to invite in modern conductors, however, they also gave modern soloists the opportunity to explore the repertoire anew. Heinrich Schiff, Thomas Zehetmair and Emanuel Ax are three examples, but it was Viktoria Mullova who made a particularly important journey in their company. She was first invited to play Mozart concerti: 'I wanted to refresh my interpretation of Mozart by playing with original instruments. It was a good opportunity for me to explore this new world.' She played her first date in Harrogate: 'I was absolutely terrified in the rehearsal. It was really scary for me to work without a conductor, and to lead the rehearsal. Just talking to the musicians was very daunting at first. The biggest difficulty for me to deal with was the intonation because the pitch was lower. I had to use a new technique for playing on gut strings. At first when I started to practise it would take weeks to get used to the pitch and the strings. Now it comes much more naturally to me.' Mullova went on to make four major tours with the OAE, and became attuned to the collaborative process: 'When you are a soloist you talk directly to the conductor. But with OAE I had to take on a new role and be more involved in the rehearsal process. Now it's much easier to talk with the players.'

Modern conductors who worked with the OAE in the latter part of the 1990s included Marin Alsop, Andrew Davis and Paavo Järvi. Lisa Beznosiuk recalls the concert of Saint-Saëns and Fauré with Järvi: 'I felt we had always worked with conductors from our own field, or conductors who were almost part of the family, like Elder and Fischer. But when we worked with Paavo, we didn't know him at all, there was that distance and it was invigorating - it felt we were being more like grown-ups.'

When talking to OAE players the concept of a 'grown-up' music profession is a recurring theme. It was to escape this world of routine and superficial professionalism that the founding members created the Orchestra. But after years of exposure to diverse stylistic and cosmopolitan influences, why did they still feel child-like? Perhaps it is a measure of the sheer strength of their idealistic desire to grow and develop musically together. Complacency has always been anathema to the OAE's ethos. As clarinettist Antony Pay remarked, OAE musicians have retained a sense of wonder: 'The most striking aspect of working with the Orchestra for me has been to encounter a renewed sense of 'specialness' as a feature of some of the great pieces of music in the orchestral repertoire. In a standard symphony orches-

tra you might perform Brahms's Violin Concerto as a matter of course. But when we did it in the OAE, it was: 'We're playing the BRAHMS VIOLIN CONCERTO!' Indeed, the soloist Elizabeth Wallfisch speaks of the 'excitement and joy' she experienced when playing the work: 'It was a whole new area of study: I dived into the world of Joachim, and Brahms, their passions and trials. It was revelatory to play it with an orchestra using the same forces as Brahms, the natural horns, the old wind instruments, and give the attention to the detail in the score, with the dynamic/balance so thoroughly spelled out by the composer, the result being a more transparent whole, where the score came to light in ways never heard in our time before.'

THE (MANY) INSTRUMENTS OF THE ORCHESTRA

For a performance of a 19th Century work, like Brahms's Violin Concerto, each member of the Orchestra takes responsibility for having the correct instrument, set-up in the correct way, a bow from the period and, in the case of winds and brass, instruments of the correct type, date and nationality. Few in the audience will appreciate the painstaking research that goes into each concert. For example while ebony one-keyed flutes are used in Baroque repertoire, the lighter rosewood, 8-10 key variety are used for Brahms. An oboe will be found within five years of the date, and similarly with a clarinet. As the players have become more experienced, some other considerations have come into play, as Antony Pay explains: 'I do play on copies of 19th Century German instruments by Georg Ottonsteiner, but I am sensitive to the notion that it is more important you find a good instrument that you can play expressively rather than a 'correct' instrument simply for its type and date.' It's a controversial area: many feel that an instrumentalist is only in a position to make such a decision if they have, like Pay, years of experience of playing on the actual instruments of the period; then their physical memory of the style demanded by the original instrument can be transferred onto a more recent instrument. Co-principal cellist Richard Lester, well-known as a Classical specialist, is convinced that the quality of the instrument is paramount: 'I think with a cello the primary factor is that you are playing a great instrument that you can play well, strung with gut, not necessarily one that is made at the exact correct date but which is actually lousy. It is slightly different with horns, for example, because the horn from each period and place sounds so distinctive.'

A subject in which Andrew Clark, one of the OAE's principal horns, is well-versed: 'We know that the earliest tuning slide was invented in the 1750s, which made the Classical period instrument more adaptable than its Baroque predecessor. After this date the music cannot really be played on the earlier instruments - you would need too many crooks and a tuning slide to adjust for them.' Berlioz presents a particular challenge for those who want to recreate his own performances: 'Berlioz was enthusiastic about the new valve horn, against the ruling of the Paris Conservatoire. It's fascinating to look at his horn parts in his *Roméo et Juliette:* there are four different keys represented in the horn section at one point. It seems he was imagining a curious blend of stopped and unstopped notes, with possibly two types of horn in mind, one stopped, one valved. So you have a choice: either you can recreate what you think he was aiming for, or you can play it as it might have been tackled by one of the many European orchestras he conducted.'

Clark and his colleagues often play on reproduction instruments since the presence of impurities in the 'calamine' brass alloy used before

Elizabeth Wallfisch, soloist in a performance of Brahms's Violin Concerto in 1994, rediscovered the work: 'It was revelatory to play it using the same forces as Brahms... the result being a more transparent whole, where the score came to light in ways never heard in our time before.'

1750 has tended to result in corrosion. Actual antique woodwinds can be found, but there was one project in 1999 for which reproductions had to be specially made to suit the unusually low pitch. This was for the Salzburg Festival performances of Rameau's *Les Boréades* conducted by Simon Rattle, who had long harboured a desire to conduct it since hearing John Eliot Gardiner's production of 1982. David Pickard remembers the buzz around this production: 'This music is so stylistically specialised, everyone focussed on refining their approach, it took three months to work on it – there was so much to think about.' The pantomime-like production, by Ursel and Karl-Ernst Hermann, drew criticism – Andrew Clements asked, ' What is the point of lavishing so much time and effort on so-called musical authenticity, when not the slightest attention is given to period manners on stage?' – but the colour and vitality of the orchestral playing, and the performances of a glamorous cast, including Barbara Bonney and Heidi Grant Murphy, were warmly praised. Rattle publicly complimented the Orchestra and gave them their own encore to play.

Lisa Beznosiuk talking to Simon Rattle.

LES BORÉADES WITH SIMON RATTLE, SALZBURG FESTIVAL **1999**
LISA BEZNOSIUK (PRINCIPAL FLUTE)

Looking back over 21 years the production of Rameau's *Les Boréades* at the Salzburg Festival in 1999 stands out vividly in my memory for a number of reasons.

First and most significantly, *Les Boréades* represented a welcome return to the repertoire which had first thrilled me when, as a wide-eyed ex-student, I sat alongside my teacher Stephen Preston in Lina Lalandi's pioneering Rameau opera performances in the 1980s. The sensuous shapes and subtle nuances which characterise French music are central to any player of the Baroque flute. It was also the first time we had ever played any Baroque repertoire with Simon, and the lavish orchestration, dramatic harmony, compelling dance rhythms, exquisite and opulent melodies made *Les Boréades* an ideal choice. His natural understanding of French style penetrated to the heart of this extraordinary score. Simon told us that he'd always nursed an ambition to conduct this work ever since hearing John Eliot Gardiner's ground-breaking Proms performance with the Monteverdi Orchestra playing mainly modern instruments.

The woodwind players had a preliminary rehearsal with Simon to test out our juicy-sounding new low pitch instruments (a whole tone below modern) and to try out a few of the more challenging passages. At a pause in the rehearsal he said (in the nicest possible way) something along the lines of 'this *really* is very difficult on these instruments, isn't it?' Pushing forward boundaries and stretching both players and instruments to their limits is a recurrent theme for the OAE and this was borne out by the resounding success in Salzburg under Simon's characterful direction.

Another reason it was so memorable was for the participation of an extremely lively and engaging French harpsichordist. It was our first encounter with Emmanuelle Haïm, whose experience and musicianship brought a huge amount to the production and whose vibrant personality left few hearts untouched. *Les Boréades* gave us a chance – alas now all too rare in this age of cost-effectiveness – to explore perhaps the most unique and dazzling work from a remarkable genre. I look forward to another fully-staged Rameau opera!

BACK TO BEETHOVEN

Les Boréades was a special event, an exploration into virgin territory, but the Orchestra regularly returned to their core repertoire to rediscover it. The plan for Autumn 1999 - to play all the Beethoven symphonies with different conductors, Brüggen, Fischer, Mackerras, Norrington and Rattle – was a compelling and inimitably OAE project, but it was going to be expensive. In 1997 Martin Smith had suggested to one of his clients, John Duffield, the former Chairman of Jupiter Asset Management Limited, that he might be interested in the Orchestra. Duffield was a great lover of Beethoven, and immediately got behind the symphonies project. But, says Pickard, 'What began as the passion of one person turned into a corporate belief. It was commercially so successful for them, in terms of the entertaining they did, the business they did, the sense of a relationship with the family of players, that many of them became converted to the whole idea of the Orchestra.' Says Emma Howard Boyd of Jupiter, who oversees the relationship today, 'I am particularly pleased to see how our relationship with the Orchestra has evolved beyond pure sponsorship, to include a partnership with both the OAE and Arts & Business on a school's education project involving over 3,000 children. Jupiter has been involved in socially responsible investment for over 18 years, and this project has allowed our sponsorship to help match our own sense of corporate responsibility.' Edward Bonham Carter, Jupiter's Joint Chief Executive points to the length of time Jupiter has been Principal Sponsor of the Orchestra: 'This has been an excellent relationship for us. We are delighted our long term sponsorship has given the OAE stability and enabled the players to develop into an artistically-renowned and world-class Orchestra, matching our reputation in the investment world for consistent out-performance.'

Both organisations were responding to a marked change in the corporate world as the Century neared its end. Martin Smith: 'There was a whole new ethos coming in, one had to look at corporate and social responsibility, responsibility to share-holders: some of the fund-raising I initiated in the early days would be much harder now.' Marcus sees the sponsorship model already evolving rapidly into a more dynamic, hands-on relationship between players and staff members of a company or the community in which the company is based. With respect to public funding the Orchestra had won an 'Arts 4 Everyone' award from the Arts Council in 1997, as well as receiving £80k to stage concerts in St. George's Brandon Hill, Bristol, a venue the OAE had originally performed in for the BBC. This was to provide the springboard for what has become a South West residency. Since the mid-1990s the OAE had received some Arts Council support for short UK tours, but in 2000 a revenue package was offered: Pickard remembers calling his Development Manager, Kirsty MacDonald (née Lynn), "You'll never believe this, but I think the Arts Council are going to fund our tours on a more regular basis!" It was a watershed moment. The OAE had been going it alone for fourteen years before that level of government support came direct to the organisation.

LEAVING A TRACE

The Beethoven symphonies project, like so many of the OAE's wide-ranging, multiple artist events, made a huge impact on its audiences and was broadcast on BBC Radio 3, but otherwise left no trace. Since the demise of the Virgin contract, recordings with the Orchestra had been more fitful and were usually driven by star soloists – Andreas Scholl, Renée Fleming, Cecilia Bartoli, Susan Graham – rather than the Orchestra's own programming. With a recession in the record industry, the lack of a single figurehead at the OAE made it even harder to get projects off the ground: 'We were glad that there was the *Così fan tutte* recording with Rattle for EMI, but it was a source of frustration that we were rarely able to make the OAE a selling point in itself,' says Pickard, 'The Beethoven series was one of my happiest memories, but how could one label have taken that on with all those different conductors?' In fact, self-recording is now becoming the norm for orchestras. Says Pickard, 'This may be the way forward for the OAE, who have a rich archive of broadcast recordings.'

The extraordinary Berlioz tour of Europe with Simon Rattle and Anne Sofie von Otter in 2000 was another project that went unrecorded, though few will forget their *Symphonie Fantastique:* 'There's nothing quite like old instruments to make it new,' wrote Rob Cowan, 'The familiar Berliozian crisis between Classicism and Romanticism suddenly seemed irrelevant, with freshly revealed key collisions, a merciless March to the Scaffold and the Finale's morbid ruckus… it was surely a defining moment in Rattle's experience of Berlioz. And ours too.' Another performance considered a benchmark by players was Verdi's Requiem with Mark Elder, late in 2001. 'Personally, I think that the Verdi Requiem was the fulfilment of our work together up to that point' says Elder. 'It was a huge step forward for the players: hearing the new bowings, new tempi, new colours made it a thrilling experience.' Oboist Anthony Robson echoes his feelings: 'Mark has such a way with Verdi, that was the most moving performance I will ever do. It was just after 9/11. [Soprano] Christine Brewer broke down in tears at the rehearsal and couldn't carry on singing: we all felt it.'

Annette Isserlis and Iván Fischer.

BEETHOVEN'S FIFTH SYMPHONY, 1999, IVÁN FISCHER
ANNETTE ISSERLIS (VIOLA)

Iván's face lights up. 'I harv an ideeaar.'

He strides purposefully to the rear of the Orchestra to communicate his 'ideeaar' to the trombone section, who are huddled in companionable isolation, as is their wont. Seconds later, he is striding furiously back, with a face like thunder.

'Vy are they always so barlardy mizzerrrarble?' he demands, rhetorically.

His suggestion had been that they should stand for the momentous trombone entry at the opening of the last movement: Beethoven's first-ever use of trombones in the context of a symphony. In the event, Iván managed to persuade the trombones to stand, and the effect was hair-raising for orchestra and audience alike.

Iván has an ability to make the Orchestra exist in several time-dimensions simultaneously. There is the structural arch stretching away into the distance, its components finely etched in rhythmic detail. There is the ebb and flow of harmonic and agogic tension serving the rhetoric. But the performance is of the moment; the music shimmers with mercurial changes of aspect, rich with inflections and elasticity so that the drama is all-pervading. He doesn't believe in rehearsing to make us feel comfortable, but rather to have the freedom to explore what might be possible. In performance it feels dangerous, exciting, integrated and spontaneous all at the same time.

In 2000 and 2001 the level of activity intensified dramatically: Roger Norrington led a tour of Mahler's First Symphony to great effect, there were tours in the UK, Europe, in Spain and Mexico, including a Schumann, Weber and Beethoven tour with Robert Levin and Charles Mackerras; Thomas Zehetmair played Vivaldi concertos, Rattle led *Fidelio* at Glyndebourne, and there was even a new work especially written for the OAE and the Birmingham Contemporary Music Group by Mark-Anthony Turnage, *About Time*. All these had been planned by the ADC in partnership with David Pickard and James Ellis, his Artistic Administrator, who was also a violinist, composer and mandolin player. But 2001 saw big changes: David Pickard had already made an impression at Glyndebourne, and that year he took up the post of General Director at the opera festival. He was succeeded by his Director of Development, Kirsty MacDonald.

BLOWS OVER BACH

One of the aims of the musicians who founded the OAE was to shift the balance of power between themselves and their conductors. They wanted to be in control of who came to work with them, on what repertoire and to decide whether they were invited back. They wanted the vision and inspiration of the chosen conductors, but they also wanted their own contribution to be acknowledged. Viola player Nicholas Logie articulates their fundamental aspiration: 'We wanted to be more than skillful technicians. When conductors come to work with this orchestra I do think they get a

Margaret Faultless

BERLIOZ'S SYMPHONIE FANTASTIQUE, 2000
MARGARET FAULTLESS (LEADER) AND SIMON RATTLE (CONDUCTOR)

MF 'I'll never forget the *Symphonie Fantastique* in Cologne with Simon Rattle. That was extraordinary. I remember coming off stage and realising that that was probably as good as it could get, in terms of what Simon wanted and what we could deliver. He is incredibly demanding, the more he gets, the more he demands. *Symphonie Fantastique* is a truly virtuoso orchestral piece and, although I felt that none of us had run out of possibilities, particularly Simon, of course, we had given a virtuosic performance to match the work itself. When you have a group of really good players and a great conductor, the result can be greater than the sum of its parts. We all hope for this, but you can't plan for it. I don't think anybody playing that night can have been untouched by the experience. It was one of those occasions that makes you realise just how exceptionally rewarding our job can be.'

SR 'It was always very exciting when we tried to conquer new ground – and Berlioz was the biggest revelation of all for me – I realised that I had been conducting a transcription all my life, since I first performed this at 17: every bar was coming up new, all the timbres were new. I was demanding from the OAE what I would demand from the Berlin Philharmonic, the ensemble, the intonation – not easy with French bassoons and ophecleides – I'll never forget the intonation rehearsal with the bassoons, one of the filthier experiments of my life! It was important that the OAE players realised that they could be that expressive, that it's not wrong to be extreme in expression. It was wonderful for an orchestra that can be so careful, so sensitive, so often dealing in subtleties, for them to be extreme – that was very healthy.'

lot back from the players, and they have to work with that contribution and make something else happen. It's a unique feature of this band: we wouldn't ask conductors back if their mode of working was just to impose ideas. I feel that everyone here has permission to BE a musician.'

Different conductors have always taken on the musicians of the Orchestra in their own style: there were those like Leonhardt with a very intellectual, research-based approach and a thorough knowledge of the sources, and those who came in from outside, like Elder: 'In the early days I had to learn how to push them, when to let go. They argued and talked and I didn't know if we were going to get things together in time. I had to teach them to read my gestural language: "Look, that was great, but I'm here too, don't wait for each other, look at me!"'

Nicholas Logie, viola player: 'We wanted to be more than skillful technicians... We wouldn't invite conductors back if their mode of working was just to impose ideas. I feel everyone here has permission to BE a musician.'

Some conductors relished the challenge of the players' 'bolshiness'. Vladimir Jurowski, who first conducted the OAE in 2001, took on *The Magic Flute* with them three years later with some trepidation: 'I knew Mozart was the OAE's terrain and I was extremely nervous before working on this, so I read all the literature – they are so well-informed, they are untypical for orchestral players, so you have to take them on as intellectual partners. At one point, I asked them to write in some phrasing marks. Antony Pay, in his extravagant manner, said to me, "We completely understand what you *want*, and that is fine, but please don't ask us to change in the parts any phrasing that Mozart put in". I found that funny – it was a clash of cultures: they play every note out of passion, and I was coming from this efficient German repertory system with my practical consideration for memory lapses!'

Jurowski had no fear of revolt: 'Resistance in an artistic way is beneficial for artistic results. Compliance is not healthy, what I want is a dialogue. These players never take anything for granted, you always have to check

JUROWSKI'S FIRST CONCERT, GLINKA AND BORODIN, 2001
VLADIMIR JUROWSKI (CONDUCTOR)

When I first heard the OAE they were playing Handel's *Rodelinda* under Charles Mackerras. The ease and virtuosity and warmth with which they approached Handel was overwhelming. I never thought at the time that I could work with them, as I was not a specialist. So I was surprised and delighted when James Ellis came to Bologna to ask me to do a Russian programme. I had long wanted to wipe all the Romantic dust and heaviness off Glinka's music. And I wanted to do Borodin's Symphony no. 2 which most of the players would only have encountered in a youth orchestra, and never have engaged with seriously. I took the *Ruslan and Ludmilla* Overture at the speed I wanted from the start – 'that was a very brave performance!' I said to them, they didn't have a clue but they threw themselves into it, for the sheer pleasure of it. It was a completely different sound and I had to adjust to the different balances. There are instruments that you think of as very powerful like the bassoon and flute that suddenly appear gentle and feminine, and I had difficulties in hearing the brass, which can dominate a Russian orchestra. We tried many ways of balancing it, and they were so open to suggestion: the way they approached it was typical of a chamber group, everything was to be explored, discussed, made new. They gave an extremely musical performance, that may sound silly, but we know many orchestras can be unmusical. It was quite an adventure and at the concert they rose to the occasion far beyond my expectations.

Vladimir Jurowski

your reasons, it's not a fight it's a creative search. It's an orchestra that is extremely stimulating: you know they will ask questions which need long, concentrated thinking before you can answer.'

Rattle has always had clear ideas about what he wanted to achieve, but enjoys a lively dialogue with the players: 'There were always more opinions in the room than there were people sitting in it,' he laughs. He is famously demanding, but when it comes to the performance, comments Alison Bury, 'I always have a sense of freedom, he enables us to play at our best, he works in the moment, and no two performances will be the same.' There was just one occasion, however, when some of the string players dug in their heels and refused to follow Rattle. The work was Bach's St. John Passion, and the occasion almost precipitated a crisis in the OAE's relationship with the conductor. Rattle met with some players in Paris and gave them the parts that had been bowed for a CBSO performance. Jan Schlapp takes up the story: 'In retrospect, we should have asked for clean parts, the bowing often went against what we would naturally do with Baroque bows, where the choice of up or down bow is integrated with the stress, articulation and harmonic tension.' It was more than the bowing though, some string players recoiled from the conductor's dramatic, even operatic approach. 'The work is a seminal one for us and we have always put it in a spiritual context, so the style felt wrong. There were many in the Orchestra who were interested in and positive about this emotional approach but some of us felt that in some way it questioned our whole raison d'être. I don't know why we couldn't make that jump to Simon's viewpoint but we didn't and that shocked us almost as much as it shocked him.'

Rattle did feel severely undermined: 'Bach is not something I would do again with them. I realised that the wind players were prepared to come with me, but not the strings. It was like trying to serve a kosher community with pork. They were saying "You can't ask us to do that". If they had been doing it with Nikolaus Harnoncourt, he would have ripped into them – but if I could conduct Bach like Harnoncourt, I would be a happy man.'

The experience with Rattle left both sides feeling shaky and bruised. Rattle now wonders if their intransigence came from having become too comfortable: 'I think there was a sense that the Orchestra was getting pretty settled, they had found something that worked well and they didn't want to be unsettled.' Marshall Marcus noticed with growing anxiety how Rattle seemed to be reassessing the Orchestra after the St. John Passion and his recent taste of working in Berlin: 'During 2002 he came along to some concerts, and I felt he was asking the question, 'Are you prepared to move on and grow or are you becoming English dilettantes? And I felt it was the right question.'

As it happened, they were booked to do *Idomeneo* with Rattle at Glyndebourne the following year: 'He came at it like an exocet missile; fortunately, the Orchestra responded, and showed they could be real professionals: it was a tremendous reaffirmation. It also brought us full circle. Our first performance with Rattle only a year after we formed had been the sensational *Idomeneo*; now another chapter had been brought to an end with the reinvigorated stage performances. In an important sense, we really had arrived: the OAE was becoming professionalised without losing its spirit.'

Taking Flight: 2002-2006

The Orchestra was booked for a season at the Châtelet in Paris in 2002, performing with William Christie and Simon Rattle, and took on Handel's *Jephtha* with René Jacobs. Violinist and Chairman Marshall Marcus took over the reigns in 2003, Cecilia Bartoli toured her ground-breaking Salieri programme in the United States in 2004 and Emmanuelle Haïm conducted the Orchestra in Charpentier's *David et Jonathas*. A South West residency was launched that same year. An important series on Mendelssohn at the South Bank in 2005 culminated in a complete performance of *A Midsummer Night's Dream*, with the Orchestra as stage, props and extras, the first staging being given in New York. The educational work of the OAE was increasingly driving audience and players' professional development. By the end of 2006, plans are well advanced for the OAE to move, alongside the London Sinfonietta, to bespoke premises at Kings Place. As Marshall Marcus leaves to become Head of Music at the South Bank Centre, the OAE launches a major ten-year artistic strategy, developed by the players.

2002 René Jacobs conducts Handel's *Jephtha*.

2002 Weber's *Euryanthe* at Glydnebourne.

2003 *Idomeneo* at Glyndebourne, conducted by Simon Rattle.

2003 Marshall Marcus takes over as Chief Executive.

2003 Violinist Thomas Zehetmair performs Schumann's Violin Concerto.

2003 Cello section on Japan tour with Masami Shigeta (Japanese agent) and Donagh Collins (UK agent).

Photos: Susan Benn, Evoke photography, London, Mike Hoban, Laurie Lewis, Eric Richmond, Alvaro Yanez

2004 American tour with Cecilia Bartoli singing Salieri.

2004 Charpentier's *David et Jonathas* with Emmanuelle Haïm (above).

2005 *A Midsummer Night's Dream*, staged within the Orchestra and directed by Tim Carroll.

2005 Handel's *Giulio Cesare* at Glyndebourne and the Proms.

2005 *Listening in Paris* series explored the changing nature of the audience from 1750-1850.

2006 *Baroque Journeys* project led by Rachel Podger.

2006 Nicholas Hytner discusses his production of *Così Fan Tutte* with the players at Glyndebourne.

2006 Bassoonist Sally Jackson features in 21st anniversary campaign.

2008 Kings Place, near Kings Cross, new home for the OAE.

Taking Flight

The year 2002 opened with a season at the Châtelet performing *Fidelio* with Rattle and *Rodelinda* with William Christie. With tours planned to the United States and Japan, the Orchestra appeared to be riding a glittering wave. Yet a combination of factors was putting the Orchestra's finances under strain. It was fortunate that Kirsty MacDonald had been a highly effective Director of Development since, when she took over as Chief Executive, the Orchestra needed every penny she had raised. Tours had become less lucrative, partly due to the strength of the pound and the slashing of promoters' budgets, and sponsorship was harder to find. Added to that, performing 19th Century repertoire meant having a much larger, more expensive orchestra: the tour in which Roger Norrington conducted Mahler's first symphony was particularly costly for that reason.

Kirsty was also finding that the job of CEO was not quite what she had imagined: 'I realised I didn't want to be an orchestral manager 24 hours a day, Seven days a week, and that's what it takes.' She charged violinist and Chairman Marshall Marcus with selling the Orchestra to venues in the UK and abroad, and he began to consult on programmes. By the time MacDonald left early in 2003 – she became Development Director at English National Opera – he was the obvious choice to take over. 'That was a masterstroke,' comments Simon Rattle, 'Marshall really knows the Orchestra and he is fearless: he was prepared to say the unsayable: that everyone *had* to develop, that the Orchestra had to be rejuvenated from within. He has shown them that they can push themselves further.' Marcus, a graduate in Philosophy and Psychology, discovered a vocation: 'If you find conflict difficult, don't get into the middle of the decision-making process at the OAE. I learnt that conflict would always be there: people will always want a complete solution, and there rarely is one. There will always be the reforming party and the traditional party, I've always been firmly in the former camp.'

Marcus had, since 1986, had a clear idea of how Enlightenment ideals must inform the direction of the Orchestra: 'Rather than start with the conclusion and work back to a proof, start with a truth, a premise and see where it takes you. It starts with the question, 'What will we do today?'.

Anna Rowe, who had formerly worked in banking at Warburgs, came in at first as a volunteer, rising eventually to the post of General Manager. From early in 2003, she worked with Marcus and the Director of Development and Marketing, Katy Shaw, on getting the Orchestra back on a sound financial footing. By the end of the season in 2004 they were once more in the black. During this time Charlotte Wadham, as Director of Planning, did a great deal to strengthen the work of the Artistic Direction Committee 'She took it seriously and really made an impact, because she had the musical knowledge and the right combination of skills,' explains Colin Kitching, viola player and librarian. 'It became more structured and accountable, and there was better communication.'

Another figure who stepped up his contribution in 2003 was Australian businessman Greg Melgaard. He took over as Chairman from Marshall Marcus, having been on the Board of the OAE for ten years. He found his business skills could be of use in a challenging artistic environment: 'I also chair the ADC and the principal players' committee where tough personnel issues are discussed. Coming from a business background, where the objectives tend to be straightforward, I find it fascinating and refreshing to ap-

ply process management to far more complex issues. I'm also working with very smart people who have a completely different take on life and politics, which is stimulating. When looking at a project, we have to see not just whether it is profitable, but whether, if it is loss-making, it will bring about a step change in the artistic standing of the organisation. I've set guidelines for profitability; with loss-making projects, artistic and financial trade-offs are important, and must be debated.'

After a year of turbulence in the administration of the OAE, the third phase in the Orchestra's development was poised to begin.

ENLIGHTENMENT FROM WITHIN

Since 1994, the Orchestra of the Age of the Enlightenment had been building a reputation for high quality and innovative education work. 'Enlightening Education' was gradually being developed by Patricia Martin and freelance animateurs, but in 1999 Cherry Forbes, an ebullient oboist in the Orchestra who had specialist training in outreach work, was formally appointed Education Manager. Her vision for the way education might grow organically out of the Orchestra's artistic plans and ultimately play a key role in developing the players themselves is unique in this field: 'We do things differently here. The fact that I am a practitioner is where it starts. Other ensembles tend to have education managers who design a project and get external people to do it. We have a core of 15-20 players who are regularly receiving training and are beginning to design and lead their own projects. Our education work involves children as young as four to adults. Some players specialise in the primary area, others are brilliant at coaching to conservatoire level. I play to their strengths.' The OAE's work has become more ambitious and wide-ranging in the last five years as more players have become involved. In 2006 the 'Play Baroque' project reached over 3000 people, as Forbes explains: 'We were looking at sound with the little ones, a dance project with deaf children, schools concerts for Key Stages 1 and 2, coaching projects for secondary age instrumentalists, and coaching in Baroque style for those who were more advanced. I think of it like the OAE star: a family of players at its centre and all these encounters radiating outwards.'

For Marcus there is something more fundamental at work here that goes to the heart of the OAE's musical mission: 'Players have an amazing skill that they take for granted. They use it all the time without thinking and there's a terrible danger after only two or three years in the profession, because of the economics, the pressure, the lack of time, that they ossify, they become incredibly good at doing what they do, but do it without any passion. Personally, I think that's the biggest crisis Classical music faces. What the education activities have done for the OAE is that they have provided an outlet for the players to continue to develop. You turn up with your instrument, you stand in front of a group of kids and you are naked, you cannot hide, you have embarked on another voyage.'

Double-bassist Cecilia Bruggemeyer knows exactly what that feels like. She has been a regular visitor to a primary school in East London for five years as part of the Adopt a Player scheme. 'It really sharpens your performing skills. Those kids will let you know immediately if you are not communicating! And it reinforces the whole idea of what a performance needs to be. It also develops one's understanding of the repertoire: if you've had to take something apart, to give children access to its secrets, that inevitably deepens your own understanding.'

Cherry Forbes, oboist and Education Manager, right, with her erstwhile teacher and colleague Anthony Robson: 'Some players specialise in the primary area, others are brilliant at coaching to conservatoire level. I play to their strengths.'

OAE players are no strangers to learning: a high proportion of them have studied in adult life, learnt new skills and taken second degrees in literature, history, modern and ancient languages. But, as Marcus has witnessed, 'the education work has a wonderful way of unnerving people, making them think again.'

One particularly satisfying project was built around a performance of Haydn's Creation in 2003, part of the six-month series *Haydn: The Creative Genius*, as Marcus describes: 'We teamed up with a scientist from Imperial College, Professor Russell Foster, and an animateur, Mark Withers, and looked at how Haydn composed, using sonata form, his own building blocks, and then we looked at how life is made with DNA. The DNA chain is composed of two lots of pairs, four elements, three of which are a given, and one of which is random, and I suddenly thought: "This is an extraordinary analogy for how Haydn's musical structures work." We gave kids three notes and they could choose the fourth, they made DNA and they made music. The structures they were using were built using the same formal processes. That was such a good project – because the ideas were absolutely genuine, it wasn't a gimmick, it came organically out of the music.'

Forbes believes in building up long-term relationships rather than wowing schools with one-day wonders: 'That's the easy option. What are

Marshall Marcus

MARSHALL MARCUS, CHIEF EXECUTIVE 2003-2006
VIOLINIST, CHAIRMAN AND FOUNDER MEMBER, BY JAN SCHLAPP

As an orchestral player Marshall always had the uncanny knack of being at the front of the check-in queue at airports when the OAE was on tour. This involved the excellent move of being the last onto the bus to the airport and therefore first off with his readily accessible suitcase so that he could be through the check-in and seated with the inevitable espresso and the *London Review of Books* before most of us had even got our boarding cards. Little did we think at that stage that he would put this strategic planning to such good use in future years.

As a violinist he was enthusiastic, dynamic, fleet-fingered and given to providing a surreptitious jazz riff at suitable moments. At his feet there was always a book, usually on art or architecture and, although he rarely appeared to be reading it its presence suggested that his mind was on greater things than up-bows and down-bows.

However, none of us could have imagined his meteoric rise to being in charge of OAE. As one of the founder members he was often involved in orchestral policy and took over the position of Chairman from Tim Mason in 1994. But it was not until he volunteered to help Kirsty MacDonald, David Pickard's successor as CEO, with artistic ideas that we began to see his managerial potential. When Kirsty left, Marshall applied for the job and was appointed CEO in 2003. With astonishing speed he learnt management skills, restructured the office, assembled an excellent team about him and continued to work punishing hours to push through his innovative and exciting artistic projects. He has in a big way helped to put OAE at the cutting edge of musical life in this country. Moreover he has often been seen at the check-in desk waiting patiently until he is sure everyone has gone through. For that and for so much else he has our appreciation and thanks. We shall miss him very much and wish him a long and happy reign as Head of Music at the South Bank Centre.

IVÁN FISCHER AND AN ENLIGHTENMENT EDUCATION PROJECT, 1999
SUSAN CARPENTER-JACOBS (VIOLIN)

Clearly it was going to be a disaster. The multitude of primary school children sitting in the auditorium of the Royal Festival Hall were noisy and restless and, without a glance in their direction, Iván stalked towards the conductor's podium with the score of Beethoven's Fifth Symphony tucked firmly under his arm, muttering and shaking his head.

The moment the score hit the music stand he spun round to fix the unsuspecting young audience with his blazing eyes and roared: 'Right! Who wants to conduct an orchestra?'

Sixty hands shot up. 'Me!' 'Oh me!' 'Please ME!'

'You,' he pointed. 'Come here.' Finger beckoned.

One little boy stood up in the scrum of twittering lunch boxes, suddenly very alone. The whole Orchestra watched as he stumbled down the steps and scrambled up on to the stage, white faced, saucer eyes barely taking in the sea of adults, instruments and music stands now facing him.

'Here you are', said Iván quietly, with a benevolent smile. And handed him his baton.

The baton waved uncertainly in a shaky circle.

'Da da da DAAAAAAH!'

The apprentice shot out of his skin.

'Well!' said Iván, 'Was it good? Was it loud enough, quiet enough, together? Hold the baton like this and make them do it again.'

Susan Carpenter-Jacobs (violin)
School children listening at an OAE
Enlightening Education event.

The baton made a slow downward path and the Orchestra burst into life.

'Was that better?' demanded the guttural professor. The pupil nodded in uncomprehending assent.

'Who is next?' called Iván, dismissing his first victim with a flick of the wrist.

For the next fifteen minutes a steady stream of wannabe conductors climbed up onto the stage to draw patterns in the air and to put the Orchestra through its paces. We played the first sixteen bars over and over again: slower, faster, shorter, longer, louder or softer as instructed by the awe-struck aspiring young musicians, much aided by the terrifying Master through exaggerated eye movements to the players and one word orders barked in a stage whisper from behind the back of his hand.

'That's enough of that!', declared the Maestro. 'Everybody on stage.'

There was a stampede of shorts, skirts and primary school T-shirts. Some players put out a hand to help the littlest ones clamber up, others surreptitiously put a protective arm around precious instruments as enthusiastic young arms, feet and elbows whirled into their midst.

'Now,' said Iván, glaring at them with his beady blue eyes as they sat cross-legged on the floor amongst the forest of violins, violas, cellos, double basses, wind, brass and percussion instruments. 'We are going to play the whole movement. It is long, and you are not going to move. Or breathe. You are going to listen and remain completely silent from start to finish'.

He lifted his baton.

And that is what we did.

And that is what they did.

you leaving behind? I'm interested in quality not quantity. We have had three-year residencies with five schools in Camden, and one of them, a secondary school we have decided to stay with longer as I feel we are just beginning to make a difference there. It's vitally important you are galvanising the staff to carry on your work.' While the OAE's educational work started small, it is now an essential part of the Orchestra's artistic planning, and can even shape the way the main performing projects are developed.

The OAE's residency in the South West, formally launched in autumn 2004, involves partnerships with St. George's Bristol, Dartington Plus, Jackdaws Educational Trust and the Wiltshire Music Centre, and another raft of educational possibilities. Already the town of Frome has experienced 'Enlightenment': 'We worked with Jackdaws on a 'Messiah' project,' explains Marcus. 'At the end there was a performance directed by Scott Stroman, with young people playing, our players, choirs of adults, kids, the lot. The church in Frome was packed to the rafters – it galvanised an entire town. It not only led to a moving performance: there is now a Frome Messiah Choir which has continued to perform each year since we left.'

AT THE HEART OF THE COMPETITION

Despite the financial difficulties in 2002/3, the OAE were to make an important international impact in 2004, not least on an American tour with Cecilia Bartoli performing the music of Salieri, which was to become an award-winning recording. The concerts had no conductor and were led by Alison Bury: 'It was one of the most challenging things I've ever done. Cecilia has extremely high standards and I had to prepare everything minutely. She performed with real understanding of the music and the texts, and she was always willing to tell us what the music was about. There was this feeling that she required 150% concentration from all of us… but the concerts were such fun. The atmosphere in the hall was extraordinary, there were two, three or even four encores and then we would watch the audience rise to its feet. It was the nearest I'll ever get to playing in a pop concert.' Another highlight of the year were the performances of Charpentier's very rarely performed *David et Jonathas* with harpsichordist and conductor Emmanuelle Haïm. The tour covered Brussels, Paris, New York, Cuenca, London and Salzburg: Haïm's realisation of the score for a body of 32 players was characterised by 'quick-shifting and lavish ornamentation'. For Stephen Pettit, writing in the *Evening Standard,* 'Music and text are perfectly aligned, melodically and harmonically, so that listening to his most moving movements is a sort of delicious agony.' The Parisienne Haïm had been introduced to the Orchestra for the Salzburg performances of *Les Boréades,* and was subsequently engaged by Glyndebourne to conduct both tours and main performances of *Rodelinda, Theodora* and *Giulio Cesare.* Another Continental conductor that Simon Rattle was keen the OAE should meet was the Italian Giovanni Antonini of Il Giardino Armonico, who conducted them in Rossini, Boccherini and the Beethoven Violin Concerto with Viktoria Mullova in 2005. Says Rattle: 'I've been trying to push them to work with other people – there are some very exciting continental groups out there who are really coming on strongly. The point about the OAE is that they have to be the best, and most of the time they are the best, but after that comes the really tough bit, to push the energy and vision onwards, to be a step ahead.'

Antonini, Rinaldo Alessandrini, Ottavio Dantonie, Enrico Onofri and Frederico Maria Sardelli have become names to conjure with as a stream of vivacious and innovative recordings flood on to the market from their Italian groups, in part sponsored by the Turin Library project to record the complete works of Vivaldi on the French Naïve label. Haïm's own group Le Concert d'Astrée, Christie's Les Arts Florissants, Freiburg Baroque, Concentus Musicus Wien and many others are all competing in the Early Music market, and many have ambitious recording programmes beyond the reach of the OAE. The presence of some of these groups could threaten the OAE's ability to tour profitably on the Continent but, in a typically positive initiative, the Orchestra has made a relationship with Freiburg Baroque, and plans to partner them in future projects. Although the OAE has seventy-five recordings in the catalogue, it is the strong relationship with BBC Radio 3 that has proved the most powerful tool in broadcasting their work abroad, as Marcus comments: 'Through the BBC and the European Broadcasting Union, recordings of our concerts have been heard all over the world, often in places where our recordings would never have been accessible to ordinary listeners.'

Sir Simon Rattle on the Proms performance of *Das Rheingold*, 2004: 'That was a great experience for all of us. I had the feeling that the music was so grateful for this treatment. It did something to the way the singers could sing.'

DAS RHEINGOLD

Perhaps the most significant and ground-breaking performance of 2004 was Wagner's *Das Rheingold* with Simon Rattle at the BBC Proms. Although they had played some Wagner before, taking on a whole opera was entering virgin territory. 'It was terrifying,' says Principal Oboe Anthony Robson, 'At times I was frightened stiff. Wagner's music is something I thought I would never have to play: there are shed loads of rests, for a start, something we're not used to, followed by exposed, nerve-wracking solos. It was difficult, we were right out of our normal environment, but we took it on, and we rose to the challenge. The atmosphere was electric.' For Simon Rattle it was the revelation he had been hoping for:

'That was a great experience for all of us. I had the feeling that the music was so grateful for this treatment. It did something to the way the singers could sing – I remember Anna Larsson realising what different colours she could make over those instruments. I went and played it with the Berlin Phil afterwards. There was I begging them to articulate more, while I begged the OAE to lengthen the phrases more!' Audience and critics alike felt the force of the revelation: 'A piece of history was made last night, wrote Stephen Pritchard in the *Observer*, '... we became the first people in modern times to hear a full Wagner opera performed on the instruments the composer had in mind... any lingering doubts must have been dispelled by the ecstatic shouts of joy that greeted the closing bars.' The OAE, and Nicholas Kenyon at the Proms who had embraced the idea with such enthusiasm, had taken a huge risk. Rattle was aware the stakes were high: '*Rheingold* was a real experiment, we had as little idea how it would work out in concert as Mark Elder had when he did a private session on Debussy once with the Orchestra. I knew the toll it took because they were so exhausted – mentally and physically – at the end of it.'

REPERTOIRE WARS

The OAE has pushed the repertoire further than the founding members might have imagined. Violinist Catherine Mackintosh says that Brahms probably stood at the edge of their plans in the early days, though in fact Borodin, Glinka, Tchaikovsky, Wagner, Mahler, Fauré and even Stravinsky (his Concerto in D) have been tackled, with future plans including Elgar's *The Dream of Gerontius*. Leader Alison Bury felt that a performance of Liszt's 'Faust' Symphony under Mark Elder pushed them to certain technical limits: 'That was rather traumatic. I felt we were hanging on by our fingernails.'

During the life of the OAE, huge changes have occurred in the modern orchestral world, a transformation in which they have played their part. When they set out, there was a feeling that the Classical territory had been invaded by the period orchestras, and that a modern orchestra could no longer present Mozart or Haydn with any confidence. At the same time, conductors such as Roger Norrington and John Eliot Gardiner were pushing their ensembles ever further into the Romantic territory of Schumann, Mendelssohn, Weber, Berlioz, Tchaikovsky and Wagner. Harnoncourt had shown what a period instrument conductor could achieve with a modern orchestra in his seminal Beethoven cycle with the Chamber Orchestra of Europe. Simon Rattle who, even before he worked with the OAE, had been experimenting with period style with the CBSO, took inspiration from his work with real period instruments, and even invited specialist instrumentalists, some from the OAE itself, to coach their modern counterparts. In time he would take his experience to the Vienna and Berlin Philharmonic orchestras. Roger Norrington, having handed over to the OAE the work of his London Classical Players in the mid-Nineties, took off to the modern Stuttgart Radio Orchestra. 'The OAE ought to see it as the greatest compliment that they have made it essential to play in this way. Since I've been working with my orchestra in Stuttgart, they think I'm trying to run them out of town – they ask me, "Which composer have you been wrecking for us now, Rog?", he laughs. But they are making a serious point: 'I remember

Tim Carroll

TIM CARROLL, DIRECTOR OF A MIDSUMMER NIGHT'S DREAM, MENDELSSOHN'S MUSIC WITH ACTORS FROM THE GLOBE THEATRE

The really interesting thing for me was to see the actors interacting with the musicians. The OAE musicians rolled in, got their instruments out, and with practically no warm up launched into playing fantastically well. The actors sidled over to me and said 'Oh no, we're going to look like a bunch of idiots! This is a group of people who have actually learnt a *skill*, what do we do? We just tart about the place, learning the odd line and posing'. They were really mortified, they felt they didn't deserve to be there.

What was delightful was the transition between that feeling and the first night in New York, when the players were then impressed by the actors and were going up to them asking 'How do you go out there and engage with the audience in that direct way?' The actors were thrilled to be reminded that perhaps they did have a skill, that maybe not everyone can do that. It was a great outcome of their meeting, that curiosity and admiration – that is rare.

Working with the OAE felt like working with the Globe, not just because they are both involved with original practices, but more fundamentally, you felt part of a mission that they really believe in. It's hard to express just how unusual that is in the world of freelance orchestras: the sense of shared enterprise, that it *costs* something to be involved. The individual members end up having been part of something special. There is a shape and narrative to the work of this band.

Antony Pay, principal clarinet:
'The enterprise of playing old
instruments must always be
secondary to the enterprise of
bringing music alive in the way it
wants to be.'

going along to hear Rattle and the CBSO do a Haydn concert,' says flautist Lisa Beznosiuk, 'and I thought it was the most stylish, fantastic playing - the cross fertilisation had already started. I do remember thinking, "Oh gosh, it sounds so much better on instruments that work beautifully." But I don't think it's undermining, I think it shows what effect we've had on the mainstream.' Margaret Faultless takes a sanguine view: 'We did have an effect on what was going on in the modern orchestral world: the barriers are down, and we should be judged against any orchestra, we don't need special pleading, nor is there a sense that we are on the moral high ground any more. There are good orchestras and bad orchestras, good conductors and bad conductors.'

Charles Mackerras, however, questions the effectiveness of some 'period instrument' techniques on modern orchestras: 'I can assure the OAE players that even the most historically-informed performance with modern instruments is a world away from a period instrument performance, it cannot ever be mistaken for the real thing. It's not as simple as some people think. The other day I was conducting a modern orchestra in a Mozart concerto and the solo pianist requested we play with no vibrato. We gave it a try but the sound was dull, it didn't sound good on those instruments. It isn't a case of taking out vibrato, you have to completely change the way you glide the bow across the string.' Antony Pay makes the point that recordings have been partly to blame in ironing out differences: 'Clever microphone placing allows technical solutions to problems of instrumental balance on the finished disc. In a concert performance, we are constantly concerned with making sure that an important instrumental line isn't obscured and the different quality of the sounds means that the problems are different ones… The fundamental truth is that whether or not there is this difference depends crucially on how the performers approach the music. In fact, the enterprise of playing on old instruments must always be secondary to the enterprise of bringing the music alive in the way it 'wants to be'. Old instruments are just a part of the unpacking of that 'wants to be'.'

Mackerras is keen to work with the OAE on the repertoire for which they have developed the appropriate musical style. 'I think the OAE is expert up to Brahms, and certainly better than modern orchestras in Schubert and Schumann, but after that they are not yet specialist: the system of slides, portamenti or audible shifting needed to perform Mahler and Elgar is as foreign to them as it is to a modern symphony orchestra; it would need a huge amount of work to get that sounding natural, the technique is quite different.'

There are OAE players, particularly the younger members, who are eager to push the boundaries of their repertoire further, provided it is with the right conductors. Principal cellist Richard Lester notes that when the OAE needs to put a larger orchestra together for late 19th Century repertoire, they can now call on younger players who come in with expertise in different playing approaches, both modern and period, and give the Orchestra the right heft for the job. Some players are more cautious: 'The OAE's range of repertoire has been both its strength and its weakness,' observes Catherine Mackintosh. 'It's a case of needing to learn a language thoroughly. If you want to do it well, you've got to speak it an awful lot. If you keep switching from one style to another, it's hard to find the time to consolidate; it requires careful planning.'

There is no doubt that the OAE's offering is still distinctive, and it is not just down to their instruments, but the particular cerebral engagement

Left: Violinist, Matthew Truscott.

of the players. Says Rattle: 'I took some of my players from the Berlin Philharmonic to hear the OAE's concert in Berlin last December and they were so moved: one violinist said to me afterwards, 'Do you think we will ever be able to play that well together?' He didn't mean ensemble, he meant the way they *thought* together, the way they all understood the music together – intellectually.'

2005: NOT JUST ANOTHER SYMPHONY ORCHESTRA

Two wide-ranging series in 2005 showed another step change in the way the OAE was communicating with its audience. *A Generous Spirit: Mendelssohn the Musician* in the spring of that year utilised the diverse talents of the ensemble, from undirected chamber music, to the recreation of Mendelssohn's St. Matthew Passion revival down to the symphonies, a string sinfonia directed from the cello by Richard Lester, Robert Levin improvising on themes from the composer's output to the enchanting staging of the complete *A Midsummer Night's Dream* directed by Tim Carroll, then Master of Play at the Globe Theatre, with the Orchestra acting as stage, props and extras. No one present will soon forget the image of Bottom, with French horns for ears, climbing into a double bass case with Titania.

Programme for the 2005 series, *A Generous Spirit: Mendelssohn the Musician*, one of several recent series exploring a subject in imaginative depth. This one included a complete staging of *A Midsummer Night's Dream*.

Listening in Paris, launched in the autumn of 2005, was yet more conceptually ambitious. Inspired by a book of the same name by social historian James Johnson, it followed the progress of the concert in Paris from the mid 18th Century through to the post-revolutionary epoch. Marshall Marcus explains: 'Johnson posed this question: in the 1750s Parisians were coming to concerts as if to a party, there was talk, dinner, fornication, often the music was incidental; by 1850 the audience had fallen silent – why? We, the 21st Century audience, have inherited that legacy: but at what cost?' He discovered by putting on these concerts and holding discussions that there was a hunger in the music world to examine this issue. 'There is a conundrum here: we have to be quiet in order to hear the music, but are we only listening to try to understand the explanation in our programme booklets? Is the audience disenfranchised because it no longer trusts its own reactions? It made me see clearly that we need to find additional ways of relating to our listeners. I think our education work has a huge part to play in this: it is the radical development centre, it can be our guerrilla force, if you like, going out there and forming relationships with completely new audiences.'

New audiences aside, Marcus pays tribute to the part the existing audience has played in the Orchestra's success: 'The fact is we have had the luxury of an incredibly responsive audience in London. That audience has grown from a small, specialist one into something quite exceptional. They have been prepared to come along with us on these journeys of discovery, however esoteric and challenging. Without their interest we simply could not have developed our programmes in the way we have.'

BACK TO THE BAROQUE

While *Listening in Paris* explored the Orchestra's relationship with its public, in the 2005/6 season the OAE players also went back to their spiritual home, the Baroque, for two significant periods of research, development and renewal. In the autumn of 2005, Mark Padmore led OAE players and singers from *I Fagiolini* in a week's exploration of Bach's St. John Passion at Snape Maltings. This time the focus was on the work as an act of faith rather than a concert drama, and the resulting performances were undirected, one critic describing it as 'a collective act of deep contemplation'. The following spring violinist Rachel Podger directed a Baroque project, involving some of the players in an intensive week in Dartington exploring the Italian repertoire, something welcomed enormously by the string players: 'It was fabulous to work with her: we need to be reminded about the speaking bow, the rhetoric, the way the earlier bow moves on the string; it all flows out of Rachel, she's so in touch with it,' says viola player Annette Isserlis. The project involved working with schools and local amateur groups and included a concert for 300 children. For violinist Matthew Truscott, a recent recruit, it has become a point of reference: 'Working closely in that environment and for a concentrated period with someone whose musical vision was so compelling was very rewarding: I felt as though our identity as a group of musicians was being strengthened and celebrated.' There are plans to make periods of exploration and training, away from the concert platform, a regular feature of the OAE year. The results of such in-depth and creative study were clear in the three dazzling concerts performed on one single day at the South Bank Centre. Says Marcus, 'We began to realise that we had several different audiences. One consisted of the young people we work with. One represented our core audience, happy with a traditional evening concert as it stands. Then there was another audience who turned up for the *Night Shift* event, who moved in and out and did not sit in *complete* silence.' The players were surprisingly affected by the informality of the late-night crowd: 'They said it relaxed them and they played in a different way. A new dynamic was at work, and it will be important to explore that.'

As OAE players know so well, audience development doesn't have to be about a flashy multimedia staging: it lies in the immediacy of the relationship between artists and audience. If there is one aspect of the Orchestra of the Age of Enlightenment that has been remarked upon above all others, it is the players' ability to smile.

Mark Padmore

ST. JOHN PASSION PROJECT AT SNAPE MALTINGS, 2005
MARK PADMORE (TENOR, EVANGELIST)

I've done the Passions several times with different conductors and felt a slight sense of dissatisfaction after each one. The conductor tends to take centre stage, but I wanted to cut through that professional polish, to rediscover the work in its liturgical context. It should be life-changing, the audience should be as engaged as the players, this is one of *the* great works of art. Normally it would be put on with minimum rehearsals, but we had a week to explore it, to listen to expert speakers, to look at different versions, to share the experience with children and generally to deepen our appreciation of the whole work. I even said 'No sectional rehearsals' because I wanted us all to be together, so the singers would learn about the bow-strokes.

I found the players very receptive to the ideas I had for performing the work. In the first rehearsal everyone had to put down their instruments and sing the chorales; they loved doing that. I think the nature of the OAE's set-up makes it possible to do projects like this. Orchestral musicians can be quite grim and cynical, because I think they are generally treated quite badly, taken for granted, disempowered. When players are treated well, when their contribution is recognised, when they are engaged and motivated, there is an extraordinary difference in the quality of the music-making.

Simon Rattle on tour with the OAE in 1994 holding Flora, daughter of violinist Catherine Ford (left).

The Future

After 21 years the Orchestra of the Age of Enlightenment is faced with a question. Simon Rattle articulates it: 'You can either be like Brüggen and his Orchestra of the 18th Century and say 'We're like an old rock group, we play till we drop and the orchestra's gone', or you can say 'We want to keep on growing'. The OAE can achieve this, but they must never become what they were escaping from. I think the fact that they are still self-critical, they are still questioning and striving proves their willingness to develop: how refreshing that they are not resting on their reputation!'

'I fell in love with them completely from the first meeting. The level of corporate intelligence was so high, and it's got even higher – the level of intelligence and response is unprecedented in my experience. We built up fiercely loyal relationships – it did become this extraordinary family. But it was never plain sailing. When we talk about this group, we talk in terms of love. There's a special bond between us.'

The word 'family' crops up frequently when the OAE is being discussed: be it a sponsor, a musician, Friend, audience member or an intern in the office, everyone I spoke to felt part of a family. That sense of family has been vitally important to a group of undeniably insecure freelance musicians: many spoke with warmth of the extraordinary support they had received from colleagues during illness, bereavement, and the multitude of ordeals life has thrown at them. 'It has been a privilege to work with such an amazing wind section,' remarks Anthony Robson, 'I continually learn from each of them, and their support has been more than I could ever hope for in life.'

And yet, there are downsides to families. Families can act as props for the weak; families can fall out, families can harbour resentments or find themselves trapped in fixed positions. Families can also alienate or reject members: there are many freelance musicians who play occasionally with the OAE, who do not feel so welcome: 'I feel like an under-appreciated lover. I love working for them and I believe totally in what they are doing' as one described it. 'I am asked to play and then I'm not for long periods and I don't know why.'

The OAE shares the same problems as the self-governing London orchestras: who plays, who is responsible? While the meritocracy may not be as ruthless as in some of the director-led groups, the twin goals of keeping standards high and nurturing a family of musicians can be mutually exclusive. Yet Margaret Faultless celebrates the determination of the founder members to find a way through this personnel maze: 'I think there is incredible diversity here. The strength of the personalities has grown, people have not been squashed, nor have they been eased out. The organisation has grown to accommodate the development of the players, which must be a good thing.' Gradually, processes have been put in place for more trials, more selection, but it has taken a long time. As Orchestral Manager Philippa Brownsword comments: 'The challenge is that ultimately artistic decisions are made by a committee of players. If there is a dispute, there is no ultimate authority. Players have to learn to act for the benefit of all.'

'Every orchestra is impossible,' concludes Rattle, 'But they have to find a way to loosen those family bonds – without losing their essence.' Susan Sheppard, for many years the co-principal cellist, believes there is a way of renewing the Orchestra and preserving its humanity: 'We have to keep on

Trumpeters Phillip Bainbridge and David Blackadder.

striving for artistically strong and humane solutions. We are all living such precarious lives, this is a terrifically insecure existence. I really feel for the students coming through today: they are already saddled with huge debts when they leave college and, even if they find work in an orchestra such as this, then they are supposed to buy the right instruments, more than one. It's a miracle they get through to this stage at all.' Elise Becket Smith has witnessed the difficulties faced by young players and assembled the Becket Collection of period instruments which is housed at the Royal Academy of Music. Several of these instruments have been used by Jerwood players coming into the OAE, and OAE principals have been involved in workshops and coaching.

Typically, the OAE have approached the question of founder members retiring with imagination and flair. Says Marcus: 'We must help our older players make the transition. They have so much to give: they can be mentors, they have decades of experience to share with younger players, they can be involved in so many ways, so we must help them to develop.' Martin Smith expresses hope that the 'unique repository of knowledge' held by the players is retained in the organisation.

THE JERWOOD/OAE EXPERIENCE FOR YOUNG PLAYERS
BY CATHERINE MACKINTOSH

In Spring 2001, Simon Rattle sat down with us after a rehearsal in Maida Vale and asked how we saw the future development of the Orchestra vis à vis its ageing population. The feeling was that perhaps not enough young players were being nurtured. This is a sensitive subject that touches raw nerves with freelance players of any age and so those of us who were the OAE's founder-members (still in our 30s in 1986) looked around and reluctantly realised that Simon had a point. In fact, a group of us had been thinking of ways to encourage a second and third generation, and Jan Schlapp and Cherry Forbes had already written a proposal for an apprentice scheme and had planned to approach the Board in order to seek funding. Thanks to a generous grant from the Jerwood Charity, enthusiasm for the plan was generated and so began the Jerwood/OAE Experience which has been running successfully since October 2002 and has introduced us to an exceptional bunch of talented young players, some of whom now play regularly in the Orchestra. Initially we hold two days of auditions where about 50 candidates are whittled down to between 15 and 19, representative of each section, who are then invited to take part in two or three projects during the next concert season.

Catherine Mackintosh

The string players join in concerts as well as rehearsals, while the wind players usually play only in rehearsals because of the more soloistic nature of orchestral wind parts. We have also arranged chamber music master classes and concert opportunities in St. Martin in the Fields at the end of the summer to give the wind players an extra chance of performing. The scheme is managed by the indefatigable Assistant Projects Manager Ceri Jones with advice and cheers from me. Various members of OAE act as mentors to our scheme participants (affectionally known as 'Jerbils') and we have greatly valued the responsibility of encouraging and nurturing the next gifted generation of players who, like us, are passionately committed to research and performance on original instruments. A wonderful effect of the scheme has been the new layer of optimism and positive energy that this new generation has brought to the Orchestra.

'Attitude' poster aimed at students: future plans include more informal concerts like the successful *Night Shift*.

Cellist Jennifer Bullock is one of the younger generation who has come in to the Orchestra via the Jerwood scheme: 'The Early Music world has grown hugely and, with so many good players around it can be tremendously hard for young musicians to find opportunities in the orchestral scene. I was thrilled to be accepted onto the Jerwood/OAE scheme, and felt welcomed, encouraged and inspired by the players: the OAE has built up a tremendous collective knowledge and skill in its 21 years, and it is wonderful that they are passing on the distinctive style and vitality of their playing to the next generation.' In terms of the future, already there are plans for a training orchestra, and many players are keen to find and coach the next generation of players and conductors. Says viola player Jan Schlapp: 'Being a good player is not enough, we are looking for the best players who also have that special intensity of commitment, that integrity, curiosity. I would not be happy to move on until I knew there were enough of those younger people in the Orchestra to continue our work.' Elizabeth Wallfisch hopes that younger players will go back to the sources: 'It's so important to keep looking at the primary sources, and not just copy what happened 20 years ago, or listen to recordings for their learning, rather than playing the works unheard, and then discovering for themselves what treasures are contained within.'

WHAT DO WE *WANT* TO DO?

Recruitment and renewal aside, the OAE have recently gathered players together to ask some fundamental questions. It all started when Katy Shaw, who was until recently Director of Development and Marketing, asked Marshall Marcus a question: 'We were considering some long term funding initiatives, and Katy came to me and said, "Look, I can raise this money but what is it actually *for*?". Together they had a brainwave: 'We thought, yes, we must ask the players exactly what it is artistically they would most like to do, and then all the fund-raising must stem from that.' And so they have embarked on a ten year plan, their most ambitious yet, derived from the players' own passions. Marcus is keeping the details close to his chest, but he will say that some inspirational ideas together with some radical development mechanisms for raising funds for them 'will provide a startling new model for how a 21st Century UK orchestra can flourish'. Add to this the fact that the Orchestra will be moving, alongside the London Sinfonietta, into bespoke premises with its own rehearsal spaces and concert hall at Kings Place near Kings Cross and another raft of exciting possibilities comes into view. Residencies at the South Bank Centre and Glyndebourne remain. The Orchestra has maintained ties with many leading conductors and soloists. Pivotal relationships with Frans Brüggen, Charles Mackerras and Roger Norrington have been cemented by their appointment as Emeritus Conductors, while Iván Fischer, Vladimir Jurowski and Simon Rattle are poised to blaze the future trail as Principal Artists. 'You look at this story,' says Marcus, 'and you see what an extraordinary journey it is that the OAE has travelled since its humble origins on a damp November night in 1985. Some have departed, but many of us have stayed with the Orchestra, and what remains is that first question, which we continue to ask: 'What do we *want* to do?'

Marcus bows out in 2007 to become Head of Music at the South Bank Centre, but his legacy will be a vivid and daring programme.

The last word goes to Simon Rattle: 'The OAE was a shot in the dark when it started, and long may that sense of risk continue. As far out as they can go is where they should be aiming.'

Acknowledgments

This book was prepared with the generous assistance and time of: Adrian Bending, Lisa Beznosiuk, Emma Howard Boyd, Philippa Brownsword, Cecelia Bruggemeyer, Frans Brüggen, Jennifer Bullock, Alison Bury, Susan Carpenter-Jacobs, Tim Carroll, Edward Bonham Carter, Andrew Clark, Mark Elder CBE, Margaret Faultless, Iván Fischer, Cherry Forbes, Catherine Ford, Simon Foster, Judith Hendershott, Annette Isserlis, Ceri Jones, Vladimir Jurowski, Martin Kelly, Nicholas Kenyon, Colin Kitching, Timothy Kraemer, Richard Lester, Robert Levin, Nicholas Logie, Ginny Macbeth, Kirsty MacDonald, Sir Charles Mackerras, Catherine Mackintosh, Marshall Marcus, Greg Melgaard, Lisa Milne, Roy Mowatt, Viktoria Mullova, Sir Roger Norrington, William Norris, Chi-chi Nwanoku MBE, Mark Padmore, Antony Pay, David Pickard, Sir Simon Rattle CBE, Anthony Robson, Michael Rose, Anna Rowe, Jan Schlapp, Graham Sheffield, Susan Sheppard, Martin Smith, Elise Becket Smith, Steve Thomas, Matthew Truscott, Elizabeth Wallfisch, Felix Warnock, Rosalyn Wilkinson.

Photography: with special thanks to
Susan Benn, Glyndebourne Festival Opera and
Eric Richmond: www.ericrichmond.net
Design: Harrison + Co Creative
Print: The Midas Press